The Changing Structure of Comparative Advantage in American Manufacturing

Research in
Business Economics and
Public Policy, No. 4

Fred Bateman, Series Editor

Chairman and Professor
Business Economics and Public Policy
Indiana University

Other Titles in This Series

The Changing Structure of Comparative Advantage in American Manufacturing

by
Keith E. Maskus

UMI RESEARCH PRESS
Ann Arbor, Michigan

Produced and distributed by
UMI Research Press
an imprint of
University Microfilms International
Ann Arbor, Michigan 48106

Library of Congress Cataloging in Publication Data

Maskus, Keith E. (Keith Eugene)
The changing structure of comparative advantage
in American manufacturing.

(Studies in business economics and public policy ;
no. 4)
Revision of thesis—University of Michigan, 1981.
Bibliography: p.
Includes index.
1. United States—Manufactures. 2. United States—
Commerce. 3. Comparative advantage (Commerce).
4. Competition, International. I. Title. II. Series.

HD9725.M37 1983   382.1'042'0973   83-9209
ISBN 0-8357-1443-8

For Suz, who was always willing to help, and for
Carol, who was always willing to smile.

Contents

List of Tables

List of Figures

Acknowledgments

I express my gratitude to Professor Robert M. Stern who provided the basic idea for this study, and for his continuous encouragements and timely insights which considerably aided its progress. Professor Alan V. Deardorff offered several perceptive comments which significantly improved my understanding of many of the theoretical issues discussed in this research. In addition, Professor E. Philip Howrey was an invaluable source, both of confirmation of ideas and of ideas themselves, without which the development of the econometric techniques employed herein would have been impossible.

I also thank Jeffrey Pliskin, Mitsuhiro Fukao, Clint Shiells, and the remaining members of the Research Seminar in International Economics for patiently listening to numerous presentations as the work progressed through its various stages and iterations. Their comments helped to make the analysis much better than it otherwise would have been. In a different vein, I am indebted to Mark Greene and Wayne Passmore for helping me tame the wild TROLL.

I am grateful also to North-Holland Publishing Company for allowing me to reprint figure 1.1 from the August 1981 issue of *Journal of International Economics,* and for allowing me to replicate several equations from the August 1983 issue of *Review of Economics and Statistics.*

Finally, I owe a tremendous debt of gratitude to my wife, Susan. Her unwavering support—typographical, financial, and especially emotional—was of far more importance to me than she can ever imagine.

1

Introduction

A great deal of public discussion is currently being devoted to the issue of the changing character of the determinants of the structure of U.S. foreign trade. There is widespread concern over some perceived deterioration in this country's ability to compete in world markets, even in the medium- to high-technology goods which have been the traditional sources of U.S. export strength. The issue of shifts over time in the determinants of U.S. foreign trade is of substantial practical importance (Stern, 1980). The recent growth of international trade and investment has raised markedly the proportion of the U.S. population whose welfare depends on external conditions. This includes those individuals employed directly in export and import activities, those who are engaged in import-competing production, and persons involved in supplying raw materials or intermediate products to trade-related industries. Given that the welfare of these groups may be significantly influenced by changes in the sources of U.S. comparative advantage, it is essential that policymakers be made aware of how these sources have changed and how they are likely to change in the future.

   Comparative advantage does not remain constant, and both the commodity composition and factor content of trade may be altered over time. Such propositions lie at the heart of the dynamic accounts of comparative advantage, such as the product cycle or technology gap theories. At the same time, there is nothing in the static long-run Heckscher-Ohlin and Ricardo theories which precludes examination of changes in comparative advantage. All that is required in the former case, for example, is some alteration in relative factor endowments among trading partners.

   These concerns arise particularly with respect to U.S. trade in manufactures. Figure 1.1 presents some descriptive evidence. Prior to the late 1960s the U.S. sustained a positive and relatively stable aggregate trade balance in manufactured goods. This surplus on manufacturing trade peaked in 1964 but declined in the latter half of the decade, becoming negative in 1971 and reaching its largest deficit in 1972. The manufacturing trade balance rebounded sharply in the mid-1970s, but the subsequent decline recorded in 1976 has persisted, with the surplus turning to deficit in the fourth quarter of 1977 and continuing through 1978.[1]

Figure 1.1.   U.S. Trade Balances for all Manufactures, Heckscher-Ohlin
Industries, and Product Cycle Industries, 1958–1976
(Billions of Current Dollars)

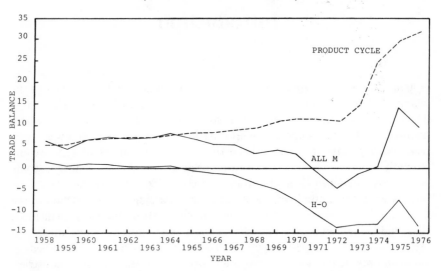

There has been some debate over providing an explanation for this decline in the trade balance in U.S. manufactures. Some observers attribute the deficits to cyclical factors, citing excessive domestic credit creation over the period as an impetus to high aggregate demand in the U.S. relative to that abroad. Consequently, American imports were large compared with exports and the problem will automatically be corrected by dollar depreciation.

While cyclical pressures may have had a bearing on the trend toward deficits, there is a persuasive alternative explanation. In particular, the recent deficits in the manufacturing trade account may reflect the existence of some long-term secular decline in U.S. comparative advantage in manufacturing. This possibility would be consistent with the fact that the U.S. has attained a relatively poor record over the last two decades in terms of productivity growth, investment expenditures, and research and development outlays.

To gain additional perspective on this conjecture, we may separate the set of manufactured goods into product groups which are determined by their technological characteristics, as suggested by Hufbauer and Chilas (1974). They divided manufactures into Ricardo goods, Heckscher-Ohlin goods, and Product Cycle goods. Broadly speaking, Ricardo goods are characterized in production by their natural resource component, Heckscher-Ohlin goods by the use of standardized technology, and Product Cycle goods by the use of advanced technology.

Refer again to figure 1.1, in which the annual net exports of the latter two product groups are plotted for 1958–1976. Net exports of Product Cycle goods increased fairly steadily until 1972, then turned sharply upward although the rate of increase was reduced by the end of the period. Apparently, the U.S. remains a strong exporter of high-technology goods, although it might be argued that the increase in net exports of these goods is related to the concurrent depreciation of the dollar. On the other hand, U.S. net exports of Heckscher-Ohlin goods declined continuously during most of the period, reaching a level of −13.3 billion dollars in 1976. Net exports of Ricardo goods, which are not plotted separately in figure 1.1, also declined substantially in the 1970s due primarily to increased imports of processed fuels and lubricants.

Further evidence of shifts in the underlying structure of U.S. trade may be garnered by examining the broad trends in the composition of foreign trade. In table 1.1 we present the value of U.S. exports and imports in total for selected years between 1958 and 1976 and the proportions accounted for by manufactures and nonmanufactures and by the three major manufacturing groups. Manufactures accounted for more than 80 percent of total merchandise exports in 1976, a proportion which has remained relatively stable over the period. Manufactures as a percentage of total imports increased substantially between 1958 and 1970 but then fell because of the sharp increase in the value of fuel imports. It is evident that the relatively greater expansion of manufactured imports than manufactured exports between 1958 and the early 1970s lay behind the trend toward deficits on this account.

It is also apparent that Ricardo goods are relatively more important in imports than in exports, although their import share has fallen substantially over the period. Indeed, it is clear that these "natural-resource-intensive" manufactures have declined considerably in their relative importance in overall U.S. trade in manufactured goods. Heckscher-Ohlin goods are also relatively more important in imports than in exports, and their share of imports has nearly doubled between 1958 and 1976. Product Cycle goods accounted for more than half of manufactured exports in 1976 as compared with around 40 percent in 1958, and for just under 20 percent of manufactured imports in 1976 as compared with 11 percent in 1958.

The steady decline in the Heckscher-Ohlin trade balance noted in figure 1.1 lends significant support to the hypothesis of secular decline. Additional evidence is available by considering the share of U.S. trade in manufactures as a percentage of industrial country exports. The U.S. share of manufactured exports fell from nearly 22 percent in 1962 to 15–16 percent in the mid-1970s. Moreover, the U.S. share of technology-intensive manufactured exports declined from 27.6 percent in 1962 to 20.5 percent in 1976, with the bulk of the decline coming in the late 1960s.[2] Thus, even though the U.S. was able to

Table 1.1. Percentage Distribution of U.S. Trade in Manufactures by Major Industry Subgroups, 1958–1976

Industry Subgroup	Exports				Imports			
	1958	1963	1970	1976	1958	1963	1970	1976
Ricardo goods	18.5%	19.0%	16.6%	14.9%	55.0%	49.0%	29.1%	27.8%
Heckscher-Ohlin goods	28.1	23.0	25.6	28.4	25.2	33.7	50.0	47.9
Product Cycle goods	41.5	47.0	50.0	51.3	11.0	13.4	15.9	18.7
Not separately classified	11.9	11.0	7.8	5.4	8.8	3.9	5.0	5.6
Total manufactures	100.0	100.0	100.0	100.0	100.0	100.0	100.0	100.0
Total trade ($Billions)	$17.7	$22.9	$42.6	$113.3	$12.7	$16.5	$39.8	$120.0
Manufactures	14.4	18.3	36.2	92.1	8.1	11.5	33.1	82.4
Nonmanufactures	3.3	4.6	6.4	21.2	4.6	5.0	6.7	37.6

increase its net exports of high-technology goods over the period, its performance in this regard relative to the other industrial countries was deficient.

The hypothesis that the determinants of U.S. manufacturing trade have undergone structural change in the last two decades has received support in the literature. Stern and Maskus (1981) reported indications of structural change between 1958 and 1976 in the estimated coefficients of a disaggregated regression relationship which was designed to reflect the neo-factor proportions theory, as defined in chapter 2. They also found some evidence of an increase in the technology content of manufacturing net exports between 1960 and 1970, using research and development expenditures as a percentage of industry value added as a measure of technology inputs. Mitchell (1975) found an increase in the labor intensity of U.S. manufacturing imports over the period 1965–1970 which was primarily due to compositional changes in the pattern of imports. Bowen (1980b) claimed that the U.S. share of the total physical capital endowment of 34 countries fell by 9 percent between 1963 and 1976, that over the same period the U.S. rates of accumulation of physical capital per worker and of skilled workers as a percentage of the labor force were low relative to other developed countries, and that U.S. net exports of manufactures exhibited a decline between 1961 and 1977 in the ratio of physical capital to labor. Leamer (1980) presented additional evidence on changes in the factor content of U.S. trade which was generally consistent with the findings of Stern and Maskus.

Such considerations lead the present study to begin with the presumption of secular change in the basic determinants of U.S. manufacturing trade, at least to the extent that such change is reflected in shifts in the factor content and technology intensity of trade. We examine this question by analyzing a data set which pools annual observations on trade and factor employments for 120 3-digit SIC manufacturing industries over the period 1958–1976.[3] The models to be considered are discussed in more detail in later chapters. Note at this point, however, that a pooled analysis is desirable. An examination of the hypothesis of secular change requires a large amount of information over a sustained time period. Since, for example, capital-labor ratios in production are sensitive to short-run fluctuations in the business cycle, inferences about changes in the factor content of trade based on consideration of a 3–4 year period may be misleading. At the same time, it is important to incorporate as much sample information from each cross-section into the analysis as possible.

This study is organized as follows. In chapter 2 we discuss some methodological points with regard to model specification and interpretation, and then review relevant studies which are available in the literature. We also provide some brief comments on the possible underlying explanations for any structural changes to be found in the econometric relationships. Chapter 3 presents the results of the econometric analysis. In chapter 4 we conclude by offering some explanations for the changes observed, and then note some implications for future research. The formal econometric methodology is developed in appendix A.

2

Specification of Models and Literature Review

In this chapter the models to be used for analysis are presented and discussed. A brief selective review of past empirical efforts at identifying changes over time in the characteristics of U.S. foreign trade is included as a separate section. Whenever appropriate, the remainder of the chapter incorporates discussions of annual cross-section studies which are relevant for certain issues of model specification and the like.

Econometric Model Specification

As stated in the previous chapter, this study commences with the presumption of recent structural changes in the determinants of the pattern of U.S. manufacturing trade. One way of confirming the existence of such shifts is to perform an extensive empirical analysis which relates measures of U.S. trade performance over time to industry characteristics which are generally thought to be important influences on the composition of international trade. In this section we introduce and discuss the nature of the models to be employed for this purpose.

We begin by specifying the major influences which are generally thought to shape the pattern of international trade. A discussion of how changes in these influences can affect the commodity composition and factor content of trade over time is deferred to chapter 4.

The cornerstone of modern trade theory is, of course, the Heckscher-Ohlin model which relates the direction and composition of a country's trade to its relative endowments of internationally homogeneous capital and labor. Since in this model there are no market imperfections and all countries are characterized by identical tastes and technologies, intercountry differences in comparative costs are determined strictly by relative factor supplies. A country which is relatively abundant in capital would have a comparative advantage in producing capital-intensive goods, and a comparative disadvantage in producing labor-intensive goods.[1]

The empirical validity of the Heckscher-Ohlin construct was called into question by Leontief (1953, 1956). Assuming balanced trade, he found that the capital per man embodied in 1947 U.S. imports exceeded that in exports, a result that, by the Heckscher-Ohlin logic, would imply that the U.S. was relatively capital-scarce. This finding was later confirmed by Baldwin (1971) among others.

The ensuing spate of theoretical and empirical work which purported to "explain" Leontief's paradox has contributed materially to our understanding of the forces which shape international trade.[2]

First, it has become clear that a simple two-productive-factor model of the determinants of the structure of trade is inadequate. A third factor, denoted as skilled labor or human capital, has been found consistently to be positively related to U.S. comparative advantage. Since the U.S. is generally conceded to be relatively abundant in human capital, this finding is consistent with an expanded version of the Heckscher-Ohlin reasoning, in which skilled labor is combined with physical capital and unskilled labor in the production process to determine comparative costs. This version has often been referred to as the "neo-factor proportions theory"; we retain this nomenclature here. Of course, allowing for a factor such as human capital implicitly asserts that all labor inputs are not homogeneous.[3] Consequently, many researchers have gone beyond a three-factor model further to disaggregate skilled labor into various skill classes.

At the same time, some authors have stressed the role of natural resources in determining the structure of trade. If natural resources and physical capital are complementary in production, and the U.S. is relatively scarce in natural resources, then international trade acts to conserve both inputs, even if capital is abundant. This natural-resource explanation of the Leontief paradox makes intuitive sense, especially when trade between the U.S. and developing countries is considered. As a result, a number of authors have taken pains to separate natural-resource industries from their data samples in order to control for this effect.[4]

From the standpoint of factor endowments, then, trade performance generally has been supposed to be related to physical capital, unskilled labor, and human capital. In addition, allowance has been made on occasion for the existence of natural resource inputs, either by explicitly incorporating them into the analysis [for example, Leamer's work (Leamer, 1980)] or by removing from the sample some arbitrarily defined set of natural-resource-intensive goods.

Newer theories of the determination of comparative advantage stress the importance of elements which the factor proportions model assumes do not exist. These involve the introduction of new and improved products and processes, scale economies, and a variety of market imperfections. It is sufficient for our purposes to provide only very brief summaries of the reasoning underlying these notions.

The "neo-technology" account of comparative advantage relies on the idea of a temporary monopoly position which a country gains by virtue of developing a new product or process. Typically, such innovations are introduced in the domestic market to exploit the advantages of better communication, less uncertainty about demand for the product, and the like. Since markets for new goods are typically concentrated in the advanced countries, this temporary monopoly position would clearly most likely be enjoyed by nations such as the U.S. In time, the new product is exported as markets develop abroad, and eventually the innovating firm or firms may decide to locate production of the good overseas as the technology becomes more standardized. Indeed, the good may be imported by the innovating country at the mature end of this product cycle, as more conventional determinants of comparative costs, such as relative factor endowments, assert their influence. Although the innovating country eventually loses its comparative advantage in this good, it is able to maintain a strong export position by continually introducing newer products, thereby procuring for itself a stream of temporary monopoly positions.[5]

The influence of scale economies should be self-evident. Countries with large domestic markets will generally have a cost advantage in the production of goods which are subject to increasing returns to scale, since, by virtue of their ability to exploit the domestic markets the producers of such goods will achieve longer production runs and correspondingly smaller unit costs than they otherwise would.[6]

Market imperfections of various kinds can affect the commodity composition and factor content of trade by altering relative prices from what they would be in the absence of the imperfections. Although there exists a wide range of departures from perfect competition which may have impacts on international trade, we mention only a few major ones here.

It is common to refer to tariffs, nontariff barriers, and psychological and geographical distance from foreign markets as resistance variables. These variables can, of course, interfere with the pattern of trade we might expect on the basis of comparative factor endowments and technological innovativeness. Deardorff (1979), for example, has shown in a two-factor model that the existence of tariffs and traded intermediate goods can alter the rankings of comparative advantage by commodity, where the ranking is based on any a priori criterion, such as capital intensities in production.[7] Much the same may be said of the influence of transport costs as well as import quotas, export subsidies, and other nontariff barriers.

In addition, the composition of trade may be affected by domestic tax policies (Melvin, 1970 and 1979) was well as by factor immobilities and other domestic distortions (Baldwin, 1971).[8]

Based on the foregoing account, we undoubtedly would like to specify a comprehensive model of the determinants of trade performance:

$$TP_{it} = f(L_{it}, K_{it}, H_{it}, N_{it}, TECH_{it}, ES_{it}, R_{it}, DD_{it}) \qquad (2.1)$$

in which trade performance by industry over time is related to the factor services derived from its inputs of unskilled labor, physical capital, human capital, and natural resources, to technological inputs such as research and development expenditures, and finally to scale economies, resistance variables, and other relevant domestic market distortions.

However, for a number of reasons, the scope of the analysis to be performed here must be more limited than that suggested by equation (2.1). In the first place, with regard to the factor services, we intend to consider only the direct factor content of the set of all manufacturing industries,[9] so that, in general, the natural resource or land variable takes on less importance. It shall, therefore, be eliminated as a separate direct factor into the production and trade process.[10]

The technological inputs will be represented by two separate variables. The first is industry research and development (RD) expenditures and the second is the number of engineers and scientists (ES) engaged in research and development by industry. These figures are available over time at approximately the 2-digit SIC level, so the inclusion of the technological variable will necessitate some aggregation across industries. The RD variable is somewhat unsatisfactory in that it represents a flow of expenditures per year rather than a stock of inputs as we have specified the remaining variables to be. Indeed, it would be preferable to consider some accumulated sum of past RD expenditures as a measure of the stock of technological knowledge available to the industry (Lowinger, 1975b and Klein, 1973). Our focus on annual trade flows and industry characteristics makes this formulation infeasible here. The ES variable presumably is free from such objections.

Finally, the remaining variables are simply unavailable in time-series form at any disaggregated industry level. Certainly the concept of domestic market distortions (DD) is not amenable to detailed measurement, and neither are many elements of the resistance variables. A scale economies variable could perhaps be constructed, as in works of Hufbauer (1970) or Baldwin (1971), but this would represent an enormous undertaking with perhaps little benefit to be expected, in view of the generally insignificant relationships between trade performance and economies of scale which have been noted in the literature. As a result of data limitations, therefore, we will eliminate these final three sets of variables from the structural econometric analysis.[11]

We are left, then, with the following two general models, choosing RD for expository purposes:

$$TP_{it} = f(L_{it}, K_{it}, H_{it}) \tag{2.2}$$

and

$$TP_{it} = g(L_{it}, K_{it}, H_{it}, RD_{it}). \tag{2.3}$$

Again, the reason for considering the models separately is the difference in the levels of disaggregation permitted by the data. All variables will be expressed in real terms to permit comparisons across years. Some comments about these models are in order.[12]

First, consider model (2.2), which is a three-direct-factor-input model of U.S. trade. It has as its intellectual foundation the neo-Heckscher-Ohlin theory as expounded earlier. However, it should be pointed out that we cannot specify theoretically correct signs for the regression coefficients for at least three reasons. First, contrary to what Harkness (1978) has claimed, the signs of the regression coefficients from some "factor intensities" version of model (2.2) cannot be said to provide an unambiguous ranking of factor abundancies for the country under investigation. For such an assertion to be correct, a complex (and unlikely) set of conditions on the prevailing technology must be satisfied, as Leamer and Bowen (1981) have shown. Second, even if we knew with certainty what the absolute factor supplies are or have been in the U.S., and if we expected factor abundance or scarcity to be the overriding influence in the determinants of the signs of model (2.2), we still would not know what to expect about these signs without reference to factor supplies elsewhere. This is merely restating the obvious: it is relative, not absolute, factor endowments which are important for the determination of trade patterns, and we should endeavor to rank all trading partners on the basis of comparative factor abundance if we wish to say anything about comparative advantage which is logically complete. Unfortunately, information about resource endowments across countries is quite difficult to obtain.[13]

Third, recall that the factor proportions theory, in any version, is of a static, long-run nature. Accordingly, for purposes of empirical investigation, it makes sense to consider a cross-section of industries in a single year. However, we are interested here in a study over time and so we intend to pool across both industries and years. There is the consequent danger of having the resulting coefficients affected by time-related influences which a long-run static theory assumes away, such as country-specific factor-augmenting technological progress and cyclical movements.[14]

For these reasons, the signs of the regression coefficients cannot be interpreted as strict measures of the relative endowments of labor, physical capital, and human capital in the U.S. This has, of course, generally been recognized in the literature. At the same time, since regression analysis is designed to relate variations in the dependent variable to variations in the independent variables, we may say that the coefficients are indicative of the characteristics of U.S. manufacturing trade performance. That is, a positive sign on the human capital input in a particular year, for example, would indicate the positive relationship between trade performance and the direct input of human capital. If the trade performance variable were some measure of net exports by industry, we would claim that, on net, the U.S. is exporting the direct services of human capital. Further, if we believe that the chosen dependent variable is a good measure of comparative advantage, then our finding would reflect the positive relationship between comparative advantage and human capital inputs. Again, the signs which result from the regression analysis may or may not be consistent with our a priori notions of how well endowed the U.S. is with the productive factors in question. If not, then either our a priori notions are wrong or factor proportions are not asserting the strongest influence on trade structure. Even so, it is worthwhile to examine factor inputs as they relate to comparative advantage, and to see how these relationships have changed over time.

Before proceeding with further comments on issues of interpretation, it is necessary to respecify equation (2.2) in a more concrete form. If estimation were to proceed on the model as it stands, that is, on the levels of trade performance and factor inputs by industry, then the results may be influenced by variations in industry size. That is, industries that are large in absolute size in terms of factor inputs may have correspondingly large absolute trade performance measures (Branson and Junz and succeeding comments, 1971, Branson, 1971). This reflects the fact that models such as (2.2) are strictly supply oriented, while industry size is dependent on demand factors as well. Consequently, each of the factor inputs must be scaled by some industry size component. One procedure which suggests itself, and which has often been employed in the literature, is to divide physical capital and human capital by the labor input so as to recast the independent variables in terms of physical and human capital per man in production. This would, of course, be reasonably consistent with the Heckscher-Ohlin notion of factor intensities.

The present research adopts a different approach. Although it is agreed that the inputs should be expressed in some factor intensity form, we consider the practice of scaling by labor inputs to be somewhat objectionable. In addition to the obvious problem of satisfactorily defining the concept of factor intensity in a multi-factor world, there is the difficulty that dividing K and H by L eliminates the possibility of identifying the relationships between trade performance and the three factors separately, as opposed to the capital-labor ratios K/L and H/L. Instead, we scale all three factors by the real value of industry shipments, S. The resulting variables then measure labor, physical capital, and human capital usage per unit of real output.[15]

These factor-output ratios exactly correspond to factor intensities if the production technology is characterized by fixed coefficients. If not, the ratios still make sense as factor intensities in the long run, and consequently their use as the independent variables in cross-section analysis is reasonable. The situation becomes more complicated in the time-series context, as will be discussed below.

The choice of the proper dependent variable(s) has been a matter of some controversy in the literature, although this debate will not be reviewed here.[16] In general, the trade performance variable selected should be scaled to account for industry size and should also be an acceptable measure of comparative advantage in trade. This leads us to choose, as the variable upon which our main attention will be focused, net exports by industry divided by industry shipments. Since at any practical level of disaggregation we find the existence of two-way trade, then empirically the notion of comparative advangtage is the proposition that the U.S. should be a net exporter of the goods in which it has a comparative advantage—whatever the source—and a net importer of goods in which it is at a disadvantage. Similarly, the factor content version of the neo-factor proportions theory is generally stated in terms of the net exports of factor services. Finally, as Baldwin (1972, p. 465) states, "... trade theory should, I think, generally focus on net trade flows ... since the policy variables in which we usually are concerned are framed in net terms, for example, balance-of-trade or net employment effects of trade policy changes." Hence, both for purposes of examining trends in comparative advantage and of making reasonable statements about policy implications, an emphasis on scaled net exports is sensible.

At the same time, a number of studies have separately analyzed imports and/or exports as measures of trade performance (Weiser and Jay, 1972, Leamer, 1974, and Aho and Carney, 1979, are examples). The current study will also make use of scaled versions of these variables, although the results will be considered as supplementary. That is, given our information on changes in the characteristics of comparative advantage from the net exports experiments, it is hoped that additional light may be shed on these characteristics by examining trends in the factor content and technology intensity of exports and imports alone. To implement this procedure, industry exports will be divided by the value of shipments. The resulting ratio, exports per unit of output, remains a crude indicator of comparative advantage in that this ratio will be higher for those industries which tend to produce primarily for export and lower for those which do not.[17] Imports, on the other hand, will be scaled by industry consumption (defined as value of shipments minus exports plus imports) to reflect the fact that domestic demand determines the level of imports.

A note of caution must be struck, however. It is quite possible that exports and imports may vary among industries, for reasons quite distinct from those which determine the variations in net exports. That is, a given level of net exports may be associated with high exports and imports or low exports and imports. As an example, given the prevalence of intraindustry trade, we may expect the level of exports and imports in many manufacturing industries to be quite dependent on the characteristics of market structure such as product differentiation, promotional efforts, scale economies, and tariff and nontariff barriers. These effects will, to a large extent, be netted out when net exports are considered instead.[18]

To summarize the discussion so far, we have essentially six models which are to be employed for analysis. They are the scaled versions of models (2.2) and (2.3) with dependent variables net exports, exports, and imports.[19] We are interested in detecting what the characteristics of U.S. trade have been in recent years, particularly with respect to factor services and technology. The results of the net exports equations will be interpreted as statements about U.S. comparative advantage, while the results of the other equations will be viewed as supplementary, hopefully yielding additional information about the ways in which the trade pattern has changed in response to various underlying stimuli.

What remains is to comment on these issues of model specification and interpretation in the time-series context. The novelty of the present study is to examine a large pooled data set in an effort to identify trends over time in the factor content and technology intensity of U.S. trade and comparative advantage. Pursuant to this end, we here state the assumption which we adopt as central to the empirical analysis and its interpretation. We assume that it is permissible to examine the data for only time-related changes in the vector of regression parameters. In other words, we postulate a null hypothesis under which no change in the parameters has occurred either compositionally across industries or over time against an alternative that parameters may have been time-variant only. The reason for such an assumption, besides making the analysis considerably more tractable, stems from our perception of what the nature of any changes in the posited regression relationships is likely to be. We might expect, for example, that influences which lead imports to depend more heavily on raw labor over time would be more or less uniform across industries. This is by no means a settled question, however, and some limited efforts to relax the assumption shall be made by performing analyses for certain industry groups.

The basic approach of the study is to identify the existence of statistically significant shifts over time in the coefficients of regression models (2.2) and

(2.3). This will be done both by comparing annual cross-section regressions and by performing pooled analyses on subsets of the entire sample. There are, therefore, two fundamental questions which must be posed in this regard.

First, is it possible for the regression coefficients to change, even if the structure of comparative advantage has remained constant? To answer this, recall first that our interpretation of the cross-section coefficients was simply that they reflect the characteristics, in terms of the direct factor content and technology intensity, of U.S. trade in a particular year. These characteristics derive from the structure of comparative advantage, especially in the net exports equations, perhaps less so in the exports and imports equations. Consequently, the cross-section regressions should be homogeneous across years if comparative advantage has not changed.

With regard to the pooled coefficients, however, the situation is more complicated. To clarify matters, we rewrite the net exports version of model (2.2) in regression form (similar comments apply to the other five models):

$$(NX/S)_{it} = \beta_{NX} + \beta_{LNX}(L/S)_{it} + \beta_{KNX}(K/S)_{it} +$$

$$\beta_{HNX}(H/S)_{it} + \epsilon NX_{it} \tag{2.2.1}$$

Then, for example, the labor coefficient in (2.2.1) will indicate the relationship between labor intensity and net exports per unit of output.[20] If we place a time subscript on this coefficient, then changes in β_{LNXt} over time will reflect changes in the relationship. There are at least two reasons why this relationship might change, however. The first is the possibility of shifts in the underlying nature of comparative advantage, which is the notion of interest here. The second concerns the influence of cyclical factors. If the U.S. economy experiences slack compared with the rest of the world, for example, we might expect imports to fall while (perhaps) net exports and exports rise. At the same time, there would be unemployed productive factors and lower levels of domestic output. With regard to model (2.2.1), we would then expect the dependent variable to rise, while the movements in the independent variables are ambiguous. If K and H are primarily fixed factors then the ratios K/S and H/S would be likely to rise and accordingly their coefficients would be positive. The effect on L/S is difficult to predict. If firms tend to hold on to their workers in the face of slumping sales, then L/S is likely to go up. If they respond with large layoffs, then L may well fall proportionately more than S. There are two features of the model which mitigate the cyclical problem, however. First, the fact that the variables are expressed per unit of output tends to blunt the wide movements we would expect on this account in the *levels* of the variables. This provides another justification for expressing the model in scaled form. Another way of saying this is to note that a model expressed in levels is subject to time-related heteroskedasticity, that is, that the variables would be likely to experience narrower or wider variations around their trends, depending on the strength of the business cycles. Expressing the model in intensity form serves to diminish this possibility. Second, the sample period is sufficiently long at nineteen years to allow the coefficients to be averaged over a number of cycles. In other words, the relatively lengthy time period involved should help to smooth out any remaining cyclical effects. For these reasons then, we shall, as a useful approximation, assume that cyclical factors have no noticeable effects on the estimated coefficients in the pooled analysis.

To answer the initial question then, the answer must be a guarded yes: our regression coefficients might change in the absence of shifts in the underlying structure of comparative advantage. However, we have scaled the models and chosen a time period in such a way as to diminish, if not eliminate, the problem. As a consequence, subject to this caveat, we intend to view the results as indications of long-run changes in the factor content and technology intensity of trade which were themselves caused by shifts in the determinants of the structure of U.S. trade in manufactures.

The second fundamental question is related to the first. If there in fact have been some shifts in comparative advantage, will these shifts be reflected in the regression coefficients? That is, are the coefficients sensitive to changes in the determinants of trade? Given the discussion in the last several paragraphs, the answer is that this is an empirical issue. If our tests do uncover evidence of significant shifts in the regression coefficients of models (2.2) and (2.3), then we may interpret this as suggestive of movements in the underlying determinants of trade. If we find no evidence of changes in the coefficients, then our conclusions become perhaps more difficult to draw. Either the structure of comparative advantage has remained constant over the time period, or some kinds of compensating variations (e.g., tariff reductions which serve to offset movements in relative factor endowments) have transpired.

In summary, the present research is designed to identify the basic determinants of U.S. trade in manufacturing goods, and how these determinants have changed, over the last two decades. It is expected that these changes will be reflected in movements in the coefficients of the scaled versions of regression models (2.2) and (2.3). On the surface, of course, these coefficient changes simply reflect trends in the direct factor content and technology intensity characteristics of manufacturing trade. How these trends may then be related to changes in the underlying structure of comparative advantage— relative resource endowments and the like—is the subject of chapter 4.

Related Studies

This section provides a selective review of past efforts at identifying changes over time in the characteristics of U.S. foreign trade. The relatively few studies which have been performed in this regard may broadly be grouped into two methodological categories: those which rely on econometric analysis to illuminate the changing relationships between trade performance and input characteristics, and those which employ some version of the familiar Leontief methodology for comparing the content characteristics of exports and imports between certain years.

There have been many studies which relate U.S. trade performance to industry characteristics in a particular year.[21] Among econometric studies, however, one of the first to examine the direct factor content characteristics of U.S. trade in two or more years was that by Branson and Monoyios (1977). They employed a three-direct-factor model (physical capital, human capital, and unskilled labor) to explain the variations in U.S. net exports of manufactured goods in 1963 and 1967 industry cross-sections. Their conclusion of relevance for our purposes is (p. 113) that in both 1963 and 1967, "human capital was significantly positive, labor significantly negative, and physical capital negative but only marginally significant in explaining net exports across commodities." No tests were performed to find out if there were any significant changes in the coefficients between years.

In much the same vein, Stern and Maskus (1981) estimated a three-direct-factor model of U.S. manufacturing net exports for each of the years 1958–1976. Their data sample was virtually identical to the one used here, and the cross-section results we list in chapter 3 replicate theirs, except for the initial model specifications. Consequently, we only briefly highlight their findings. With all variables scaled for heteroskedasticity, the regressions yielded a positive and significant sign on human capital throughout, a negative and significant sign for physical capital in almost all years, and a negative and significant sign on unskilled labor except in 1958–1959. The authors performed explicit tests for structural change in the regression coefficients, and determined that the unskilled labor coefficient was significantly more negative in 1976 relative to 1958.

In addition, the authors employed a different measure of human capital, based on skill classes as measured by educational attainment, in the census years 1960 and 1970, along with technological variables such as the number of scientists and engineers as a percentage of employment and research and development expenditures as a percentage of industry value added. All these variables performed as expected in one or both years, leading to the conclusion that both factor proportions and Product Cycle influences are significant determinants of U.S. comparative advantage.

Aho and Carney (1979) conducted a disaggregated analysis to determine whether there had been a change in the pattern and composition of U.S. trade in manufactures from the mid-1960s to 1974–1976. Their objective was to analyze the changes over time in the characteristics of U.S. manufacturing exports and imports. Their analysis of changes in the trade structure was conducted by means of cross-section regressions with various measures of trade patterns or performance as dependent variables and nine industry characteristics as independent variables.

The results for the U.S. may be summarized as follows. The human capital variable was not significant in any of the export or net export regressions. This is counter to the results of practically every other multi-factor study of U.S. comparative advantage and, it would seem, must be considered an anomaly perhaps unique to their data set. Also unexpected were the significant positive relationships between unskilled labor and both the levels and changes in the levels of exports, net exports, and revealed comparative advantage. Further, labor was significantly negatively related to imports in the early sample periods. Aho and Carney described these results as enigmatic and gave no explanations for them.[22]

U.S. imports were found to be relatively capital-intensive throughout the period. Net exports, export growth, and revealed comparative advantage all exhibited significant negative coefficients, however, and this apparent U.S. comparative disadvantage in capital-intensive products seemed to increase over time. On the other hand, U.S. exports and net exports were consistently intensive in research and development throughout. This relationship was stable.[23]

In his dissertation, Bowen (1980a) sought to examine the empirical relevance of the Product Cycle model as an explanation of trade structure and as a basis for the dynamic evolution of trade. Employing a multi-country model he identified commodities as being at some stage on the product cycle by virtue of their "price responsiveness" or calculated elasticities. With this classification, Bowen then related net exports of the goods to industry characteristics in different time periods, noting that the optimal factor mix is expected to change over the product cycle from skilled labor-intensive to physical capital- and unskilled labor-intensive.

The results in this regard were largely negative, and the author interpreted this as a refutation of the Product Cycle model as an important determinant of the dynamic structure of trade and comparative advantage. Instead, he noted the important role of changes in the accumulation and distribution of productive factors.

This consideration led Bowen (1980b) to investigate the changing patterns of resource abundance and the relationship between these changes and the changes in the composition of trade in manufactured goods for a sample of 34 countries, with special reference to the U.S., over the period from 1963 to 1975. It appears that the U.S. share of the world's physical capital endowment declined in this period, reflecting a relatively low capital accumulation rate. Japan and the "newly industrializing countries" (such as Mexico, Korea, and Hong Kong) experienced rising capital shares. The U.S. increased its endowment of skilled labor, at least relative to the developing countries.

Further analysis suggested that changes in the resource structure across countries strongly influenced the factor content of world trade.

In addition to these econometric studies, a number of authors have investigated the question of changes in the structure of U.S. trade by means of the familiar Leontief technique of comparing the total factor content of exports and imports at different points in time.[24] Weiser (1968), for example, confirmed the continued existence of the Leontief paradox in 1962, showing that more labor was required in an average million dollars of U.S. exports than in an average million dollars of import-competing production. He also sought to decompose the change in the labor content ratios between the years 1947 and 1962 into a part due to shifts in labor-output ratios, a part due to changes in the trade pattern, and a residual denoted as the interaction component. The results indicated first, that the ratio of labor requirements of exports to imports declined between 1947 and 1962, although this decline was insufficient to reverse the paradox, and second, that this decline was approximately equally attributable to changes in technology and to changes in the trade pattern.

Mitchell (1975) found an increase in the labor intensity of U.S. manufacturing imports over the period 1965–1970 which was primarily due to compositional changes in the pattern of imports. Finally, Stern and Maskus (1981) performed input-output analyses of the structure of U.S. foreign trade in the years 1958 and 1972, incorporating unskilled labor, physical capital, and human capital into the factor requirements calculations. They concluded that the Leontief paradox held for 1958 but not for 1972. Indeed, in 1972 U.S. net exports were intensive in both physical and human capital in terms of total factor requirements, and there was evidence that the U.S. may have become more abundant in physical capital relative to human capital between 1958 and 1972.

We have thus reviewed the various empirical findings which have relevance for the present study. The picture which emerges seems to be one in which U.S. comparative advantage either has increased or has been maintained with some degree of leveling off in the skill-intensive and high-technology goods, comparative disadvantage has been increasingly associated with raw labor, while trends in the influence of physical capital have been unclear. In chapter 3 we will perform pooled, disaggregated analyses of these questions in order to confirm or refute the above findings.[25]

3

Results of Estimation and Testing for Structural Change

This chapter presents the results of model estimation and the structural change tests. In section 1 we briefly reiterate the model and describe the variables included for analysis. We then present the annual cross-section parameter estimates and the simple tests for changes in these coefficients over time. Section 2 reports the results of the simple tests for changes in the pooled parameter estimates. Section 3 contains the results of the modified CUSUM tests. Section 4 extends the analysis by considering two subsets of the aggregate collection of industries. The final section repeats the analysis on the models which include technological inputs.

Cross-Section Regressions on Factor Inputs

As explained in chapter 2, the research begins with a three-direct-factor-input model of U.S. manufacturing trade:

$$TP_{it} = f((L/S)_{it},(K/S)_{it},(H/S)_{it}) + \epsilon_{it} \qquad (3.1)$$

in which some annual measure of trade performance by industry is regressed on scaled direct inputs of unskilled labor, physical capital, and human capital. We first adopt net exports scaled by industry shipments as the dependent variable, and then consider scaled exports and imports separately.

Data for all these variables were constructed for 120 3-digit SIC industries for the period 1958–1976. For details, see appendix C, which lists data sources. Briefly, L_{it} is total industry employment and K_{it} is each industry's stock of physical capital, unadjusted for vintages and depreciation. The stock of human capital was calculated, following Branson and Monoyios (1977), as the discounted industry-wage differential:

$$H_{it} = (\overline{W}_{it} - \tilde{W}_t)L_{it}/.10 \qquad (3.2)$$

where W_{it} is the average wage for each industry at time t, $\tilde{W}_t$ is the median annual wage for all workers with 8 years or less of education, L_{it} is industry employment, and the rate of discount chosen is 10 percent. In order to permit comparisons across years, all variables were expressed in constant (1967) prices.

It should be pointed out at this juncture that regression analysis is clouded by the possibility of excluded relevant explanatory variables. In general, coefficient estimates will be biased and inconsistent if relevant explanatory variables are omitted which are at the same time correlated with the included explanatory variables. Our analysis will assume that no such correlation exists; this is an assumption which cannot easily be assessed in the present context due to severe data limitations. However, appendix B presents the results of some experiments which may be relevant in this regard.

Our annual scaled cross-section regressions for models (3.1) are presented in tables 3.1, 3.2, and 3.3, which correspond to dependent variables net exports (NX), exports (X), and imports (M), respectively. We pointed out earlier that the scaling factor is important, since regressions on the unscaled levels of the variables in models (3.1) would likely be subject to heteroskedasticity. At the same time, the scaled models (3.1), which are the theoretically appropriate specifications, may themselves be subject to heteroskedasticity.[1] Accordingly, we first estimated equations (3.1) for each annual cross-section and tested for the presence of heteroskedasticity. In almost all cases, it turned out that scaling by the real value of shipments was sufficient to eliminate the problem. Consequently, no further correction factors were employed.[2]

Because it was desired to maintain strict comparability of the separate annual data sets for purposes of the pooled tests for structural change, the results of which are presented later, we restricted the analysis to the 120 industries for which data on all variables were available for each year. The levels of significance are indicated as *(.10), **(.05), and ***(.01), and t-values are reported in parentheses.

The three-direct-factor-input model performed reasonably well in explaining a portion of the variation of annual manufacturing net exports. The human capital variable was positive and highly significant throughout, no doubt reflecting the relative abundance of this factor in the U.S. The physical capital variable was negative in almost all years, although generally insignificant. This finding may be indicative of some weak presence of the Leontief paradox. Finally, the employment variable was significantly negative in all years, suggesting some relative scarcity of unskilled labor.

Examining table 3.2, it is evident that U.S. manufacturing exports were characterized by their human capital intensity throughout most of the period. Industries with high imports, on the other hand, made relatively little use of human capital in production. The influence of the employment variable was just the opposite, with high imports industries exhibiting an intensive use of

Table 3.1. Regressions for Industry Cross-Sections with Scaled U.S. Net Exports as Dependent Variable, 1958–1976 (N = 120)

Year	C	L	K	H	R^2	F
1958	-.008 (0.70)	-.350 * (1.82)	-.027 * (1.96)	.032 *** (4.07)	.14	6.38 ***
1959	.001 (0.07)	-.539 ** (2.36)	-.055 *** (2.88)	.036 *** (3.74)	.12	5.11 ***
1960	.010 (0.68)	-.731 *** (2.86)	-.033 (1.54)	.032 *** (3.17)	.09	3.62 **
1961	.006 (0.41)	-.628 *** (2.77)	-.031 (1.50)	.032 *** (3.34)	.09	3.91 **
1962	.003 (0.16)	-.825 *** (3.02)	-.039 (1.58)	.038 *** (3.46)	.10	4.32 ***
1963	.012 (0.75)	-1.15 *** (3.84)	-.037 (1.57)	.042 *** (3.99)	.13	6.02 ***
1964	.010 (0.61)	-1.20 *** (3.65)	-.034 (1.36)	.041 *** (3.75)	.12	5.35 ***
1965	.007 (0.35)	-1.70 *** (3.58)	-.039 (1.39)	.038 *** (3.75)	.12	5.16 ***
1966	-.000 (0.16)	-1.60 *** (3.42)	-.036 (1.23)	.053 *** (3.61)	.11	4.80 ***
1967	.005 (0.32)	-1.75 *** (3.80)	-.021 (0.90)	.049 *** (3.74)	.12	5.46 ***
1968	.004 (0.20)	-2.09 *** (4.30)	-.024 (0.92)	.056 *** (4.15)	.15	6.93 ***
1969	-.001 (0.03)	-1.97 *** (3.88)	-.021 (0.71)	.050 *** (3.73)	.13	5.73 ***
1970	.001 (0.04)	-2.58 *** (4.21)	-.007 (0.21)	.056 *** (3.55)	.14	6.53 ***
1971	-.010 (0.35)	-2.69 *** (3.35)	-.011 (0.26)	.057 *** (2.90)	.10	4.16 ***
1972	-.029 (0.58)	-2.89 *** (2.76)	-.017 (0.42)	.068 ** (2.48)	.08	3.52 **
1973	-.004 (0.09)	-3.30 *** (3.45)	-.036 (0.89)	.067 ** (2.60)	.11	4.84 ***
1974	-.049 (0.94)	-2.96 *** (2.99)	.009 (0.18)	.075 *** (3.01)	.12	5.13 ***
1975	-.036 (0.81)	-3.47 *** (3.56)	.009 (0.23)	.072 *** (3.69)	.16	7.15 ***
1976	-.012 (0.28)	-4.96 *** (5.08)	-.012 (0.30)	.077 *** (4.23)	.22	10.88 ***

Table 3.2.   Regressions for Industry Cross-Sections with Scaled U.S. Exports as Dependent Variable, 1958–1976 (N = 120)

Year	C	L	K	H	R	F
1958	.032 *** (4.44)	−.184 (1.53)	.020 ** (2.37)	.010 ** (2.00)	.14	6.44 ***
1959	.042 *** (5.92)	−.403 *** (3.54)	.017 * (1.75)	.011 ** (2.32)	.14	6.49 ***
1960	.051 *** (5.87)	−.511 *** (3.50)	.031 ** (2.49)	.008 (1.43)	.16	7.11 ***
1961	.039 *** (4.06)	−.267 ** (1.90)	.029 ** (2.21)	.007 (1.23)	.09	3.80 **
1962	.042 *** (4.40)	−.411 *** (2.91)	.024 * (1.88)	.012 ** (2.07)	.12	5.30 ***
1963	.050 *** (5.97)	−.564 *** (3.63)	.020 (1.64)	.011 ** (2.11)	.14	6.40 ***
1964	.053 *** (5.91)	−.668 *** (3.80)	.019 (1.41)	.014 ** (2.39)	.15	6.63 ***
1965	.056 *** (6.56)	−.922 *** (4.40)	.019 (1.49)	.019 *** (2.85)	.18	8.44 ***
1966	.055 *** (6.82)	−.822 *** (4.29)	.020 * (1.72)	.016 ** (2.61)	.18	8.50 ***
1967	.061 *** (7.26)	−1.05 *** (4.66)	.020 * (1.68)	.018 *** (2.90)	.20	9.60 ***
1968	.062 *** (7.10)	−1.05 *** (4.37)	.020 (1.58)	.018 *** (2.67)	.18	8.58 ***
1969	.061 *** (7.07)	−1.02 *** (4.54)	.019 (1.45)	.018 *** (3.03)	.18	8.72 ***
1970	.068 *** (6.31)	−1.12 *** (3.90)	.030 * (1.92)	.015 ** (2.09)	.17	7.70 ***
1971	.065 *** (6.40)	−1.17 *** (4.01)	.017 (1.09)	.019 *** (2.69)	.15	7.00 ***
1972	.035 * (1.94)	−.859 ** (2.27)	.070 *** (4.86)	.015 (1.54)	.26	13.46 ***
1973	.056 ** (2.41)	−1.06 ** (2.28)	.063 *** (3.18)	.015 (1.17)	.15	6.92 ***
1974	.054 ** (2.08)	−1.06 ** (2.16)	.062 ** (2.48)	.021 * (1.71)	.13	5.70 ***
1975	.051 ** (2.18)	−1.41 *** (2.76)	.039 * (1.98)	.031 *** (3.01)	.16	7.43 ***
1976	.062 *** (3.06)	−1.32 *** (2.87)	.015 (0.79)	.027 *** (3.13)	.12	5.50 ***

Table 3.3. Regressions for Industry Cross-Sections with Scaled U.S. Imports as Dependent Variable, 1958–1976 (N = 120)

Year	C	L	K	H	R^2	F
1958	.035 *** (4.72)	.184 (1.48)	.039 *** (4.38)	-.019 *** (3.88)	.22	10.72 ***
1959	.036 *** (3.66)	.130 (0.81)	.055 *** (4.08)	-.020 *** (2.92)	.14	6.10 ***
1960	.037 *** (3.53)	.189 (1.09)	.054 *** (3.65)	-.020 *** (2.90)	.11	4.99 ***
1961	.030 *** (2.83)	.321 ** (2.08)	.051 *** (3.55)	-.021 *** (3.22)	.12	5.45 ***
1962	.035 *** (2.91)	.303 * (1.68)	.051 *** (3.15)	-.020 *** (2.80)	.10	4.21 ***
1963	.035 *** (3.06)	.465 ** (2.22)	.048 *** (2.93)	-.025 *** (3.39)	.11	4.56 ***
1964	.039 *** (3.35)	.429 * (1.88)	.045 ** (2.60)	-.023 *** (2.96)	.08	3.53 **
1965	.044 *** (3.43)	.608 * (1.94)	.048 ** (2.58)	-.030 *** (3.05)	.09	3.65 **
1966	.048 *** (3.78)	.608 ** (2.00)	.047 ** (2.47)	-.030 *** (3.12)	.09	3.65 **
1967	.050 *** (4.07)	.532 (1.60)	.035 ** (2.06)	-.024 ** (2.57)	.06	2.54 *
1968	.053 *** (4.19)	.771 ** (2.19)	.038 ** (2.01)	-.029 *** (3.02)	.08	3.16 **
1969	.054 *** (3.90)	.726 ** (2.02)	.035 * (1.69)	-.025 *** (2.65)	.06	2.45 *
1970	.056 *** (3.79)	1.06 *** (2.65)	.042 * (1.94)	-.032 *** (3.10)	.08	3.38 **
1971	.058 *** (3.83)	1.21 *** (2.78)	.038 * (1.66)	-.032 *** (2.96)	.08	3.17 **
1972	.041 (1.51)	1.68 *** (2.95)	.085 *** (3.94)	-.039 *** (2.66)	.15	6.96 ***
1973	.046 (1.61)	1.68 *** (2.95)	.084 *** (3.51)	-.037 ** (2.37)	.14	6.14 ***
1974	.072 ** (2.30)	1.52 ** (2.58)	.062 ** (2.07)	-.038 ** (2.59)	.09	3.82 **
1975	.067 ** (2.33)	1.49 ** (2.37)	.039 (1.62)	-.029 ** (2.34)	.07	2.84 **
1976	.065 ** (2.38)	2.24 *** (3.57)	.024 (0.92)	-.031 *** (2.63)	.11	4.75 ***

unskilled labor and high exports industries being characterized by a negative relationship between exports and raw labor. These findings accord with the general perception of U.S. exports of manufactures as being concentrated in high-wage, skill-intensive industries, and U.S. manufacturing imports as being concentrated in low-wage, labor-intensive industries.

It is clear that both imports and exports were characterized by a positive dependence on physical capital in production, although this relationship was perhaps stronger for imports. To the extent that the Leontief paradox was operative, then, it apparently asserted itself through a stronger influence of capital on U.S. manufacturing imports than on exports.

In summary, it appears that the three-direct-factor model of the structure of U.S. net exports of manufactures is borne out for most of the annual data samples. When the model is applied to manufacturing exports and imports separately, the results continue to bear out our expectations. U.S. exports made strong direct use of human capital in production, but tended to rely negatively on the input of raw labor, as measured by industry employment. The manufactured goods which the U.S. imported over the period were marked by their direct raw labor and physical capital content, but depended negatively on human capital.

At issue here, however, is whether there were any significant changes in the regression coefficients over the period. For example, note that the coefficient on labor in table 3.1 declined from $-.350$ in 1958 to -4.96 in 1976, a fourteen-fold increase in absolute magnitude. In order to get some information in this regard, we performed simple dummy-variable tests and F-tests to check for significant changes over time, both in the individual coefficients and in the overall regressions. The results are presented in table 3.4.

The three equations in each set of equations represent, in order, comparisons between the years 1958 and 1968, 1958 and 1976, and 1968 and 1976 for the scaled dependent variables which are indicated. It is clear from equations (3.3) through (3.5) that U.S. manufacturing net exports made progressively less use of raw labor inputs over the period, with this trend apparently more concentrated in the late 1960s and early 1970s. In addition, the human capital intensity of net exports rose somewhat over the period as measured by our coefficients. Similarly, there is evidence that exports became less unskilled labor-intensive over the course of the period while simultaneously becoming more intensive in human capital. The declining trend in the raw labor coefficient was more pronounced in the early half of the period. The production of imports, on the other hand, came to be increasingly characterized by the direct use of raw labor between 1958 and 1976. There were no indications of changes in the physical capital characteristics of any of the dependent variables.

Table 3.4. Tests for Coefficient Changes between Selected Pairs of Annual Cross-Section Regressions

Eq. No.	Comparison	C	L	K	H	DUMC	DUML	DUMK	DUMH	R^2	F	F^1
					Dependent Variable Net Exports							
(3.3)	58,68	-.008 (0.68)	-.350 (1.76)[3]	-.027 (1.90)[3]	.032 (3.94)[5]	.012 (0.56)	-1.75 (3.41)[5]	.003 (0.11)	.024 (1.58)	.16	6.23[5]	5.17[5]
(3.4)	58,76	-.008 (0.50)	-.350 (1.29)	-.027 (1.39)	.032 (2.88)[5]	-.004 (0.10)	-4.61 (5.47)[5]	.015 (0.38)	.046 (2.47)[4]	.21	8.94[5]	12.25[5]
(3.5)	68,76	.004 (0.15)	-2.09 (3.18)[5]	-.024 (0.68)	.056 (3.07)[5]	-.015 (0.36)	-2.86 (2.74)[5]	.012 (0.24)	.021 (0.90)	.20	8.45[5]	6.47[5]
					Dependent Variable Exports							
(3.6)	58,68	.032 (4.80)[5]	-.184 (1.65)[3]	.020 (2.57)[4]	.010 (2.16)[4]	.030 (2.58)[4]	-.869 (3.03)[5]	-.000 (0.02)	.008 (0.94)	.16	6.28[5]	3.61[5]
(3.7)	58,76	.032 (3.81)[5]	-.184 (1.31)	.020 (2.04)[4]	.010 (1.71)[3]	.030 (1.52)	-1.14 (2.63)[5]	-.005 (0.26)	.017 (1.82)[3]	.17	6.76[5]	2.56[4]
(3.8)	68,76	.062 (5.44)[5]	-1.05 (3.34)[5]	.020 (1.21)	.018 (2.04)[4]	.000 (0.00)	-.271 (0.54)	-.005 (0.21)	.009 (0.82)	.18	7.40[5]	0.20
					Dependent Variable Imports							
(3.9)	58,68	.035 (4.30)[5]	.184 (1.34)	.039 (3.98)[5]	-.019 (3.53)[5]	.018 (1.28)	.587 (1.66)[3]	-.002 (0.08)	-.010 (0.95)	.16	6.28[5]	3.84[5]
(3.10)	58,76	-.035 (3.35)[5]	.184 (1.05)	.039 (3.11)[5]	-.019 (2.75)[5]	.031 (1.23)	2.07 (3.80)[5]	-.015 (0.60)	-.011 (0.96)	.20	8.53[5]	13.07[5]
(3.11)	68,76	.053 (3.37)[5]	.771 (1.76)[3]	.038 (1.61)	-.029 (2.43)[4]	.012 (0.43)	1.47 (2.12)[4]	-.013 (0.41)	-.001 (0.09)	.12	4.63[5]	6.75[5]

3 = significant at the .10 level; 4 = significant at the .05 level; 5 = significant at the .01 level.

The final column of table 3.4 lists the results of testing for change in the overall regression relationships between the years indicated. The significance of the F^1 statistics gives clear indications of structural change in all three sets of equations.

Results of Simple Tests for Pooled Coefficient Changes

We begin our pooled analysis of time-related structural change in regression equations (3.1) by means of the simple tests outlined in appendix A. In particular, in this section we present the results of the pooled cross-section and time-series versions of the Quandt maximum likelihood and F-test procedures, along with some simple dummy-variable specifications.[3]

Figure 3.1 depicts the log-likelihood ratios which resulted from application of the Quandt maximum likelihood technique to the pooled transformed data set, incorporating industry net exports, exports, and then imports as dependent variables. Global minima occurred in 1969 for all three experiments. The smooth appearances of the net exports and imports paths, at least in the vicinity of their minima, indicates the gradual character of the shifts in the direct factor content of manufacturing trade over the course of the period. The exports path is somewhat more jagged, however.[4] Finally, the large negative magnitudes of the log-likelihood ratios is suggestive of the greater likelihood that the alternative hypothesis of the existence of structural change is true.

In table 3.5 we present the results of our tests for changes in the coefficients between pooled sub-samples. The columns are analogous to those in table 3.4, except that, by virtue of the autocorrelation transformations, there is no longer a constant term in the generalized least squares matrix. We denote the transformed constant term as TC.

Equations (3.12), (3.15), and (3.18) list the regression coefficients which result from pooling across all industries and all years. The increases in the t-ratios of these coefficients, relative to those in tables 3.1–3.3, are indicative of the improved precision of the estimates we get from incorporating substantially more sample information.[5]

The signs of the coefficients were consistent with those of the annual scaled regressions, bearing out our previous findings. That is, when we substantially increase the size of the data sample by pooling across all industries and years, we find that the three-direct-factor-input model continues to explain a significant portion of manufacturing net exports, exports, and imports. In addition, the signs of the coefficients accord with our a priori notions of the characteristics of U.S. comparative advantage.

The five remaining equations present the results of the simple pooled tests for structural change. As before, manufacturing net exports made significantly

Figure 3.1.   Log-Likelihood Ratios

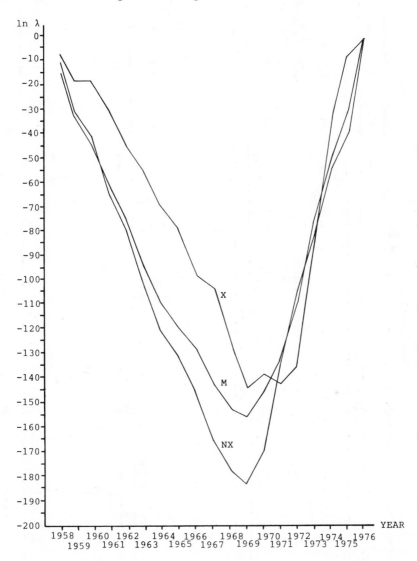

less use of unskilled labor over the course of the period, and the larger magnitude of DUML in (3.14) than in (3.13) confirms somewhat that this trend was more pronounced in the later years. In addition, the pooled analysis gave strong evidence of an increasing tendency for net exports to be characterized by the input of human capital. Equations (3.16) and (3.17) strongly suggest that the direct factor content of American exports underwent change as well,

Table 3.5. Tests for Coefficient Changes among Selected Pooled Sub-Samples

Eq. No.	t	TC	L	K	H	DUMTC	DUML	DUMK	DUMH	R^2	F	F^1 ln λ
				Dependent Variable Net Exports								
(3.12)	..	-.027 (6.11)[5]	-.643 (8.48)[5]	-.019 (3.14)[5]	.032 (11.22)[5]	....	....	....	....	.07	41.1[5]	....
(3.13)	69	-.013 (2.68)[5]	-.498 (5.82)[5]	-.028 (4.06)[5]	.030 (8.89)[5]	-.004 (0.44)	-2.45 (10.62)[5]	.001 (0.10)	.036 (5.74)[5]	.13	44.2[5]	42.8[5] -183.6
(3.14)	73	-.020 (4.51)[5]	-.563 (7.07)[5]	-.024 (3.89)[5]	.030 (9.97)[5]	.002 (0.09)	-3.43 (8.50)[5]	.003 (0.16)	.046 (5.10)[5]	.11	34.9[5]	27.0[5] -82.8
				Dependent Variable Exports								
(3.15)	..	.040 (18.13)[5]	-.542 (14.23)[5]	.045 (15.19)[5]	.011 (7.66)[5]	....	....	....	....	.50	577.7[5]	....
(3.16)	69	.035 (13.49)[5]	-.363 (8.14)[5]	.039 (10.91)[5]	.008 (4.25)[5]	.026 (4.75)[5]	-.854 (7.08)[5]	.013 (2.10)[4]	.008 (2.58)[4]	.52	308.9[5]	20.2[5] -145.2
(3.17)	73	.037 (16.26)[5]	-.439 (10.70)[5]	.045 (14.21)[5]	.008 (4.87)[5]	.028 (2.93)[5]	-.853 (4.20)[5]	.001 (0.13)	.011 (2.52)[4]	.51	300.1[5]	11.67[5] -84.0
				Dependent Variable Imports								
(3.18)	..	.061 (18.45)[5]	.053 (0.95)	.044 (10.64)[5]	-.014 (6.34)[5]	....	....	....	....	.38	346.3[5]	....
(3.19)	69	.047 (12.49)[5]	.162 (2.53)[4]	.048 (9.66)[5]	-.019 (6.92)[5]	.020 (2.58)[4]	.943 (5.52)[5]	.005 (0.62)	-.009 (2.00)[4]	.42	205.1[5]	37.8[5] -156.0
(3.20)	73	.055 (16.14)[5]	.121 (2.05)[4]	.049 (11.13)[5]	-.017 (7.28)[5]	.016 (1.17)	1.52 (5.16)[5]	-.006 (0.51)	-.012 (1.94)[3]	.40	193.2[5]	25.4[5] -79.2

3 = significant at the .10 level; 4 = significant at the .05 level; 5 = significant at the .01 level.

tending to move away from the input of raw labor and toward the use of physical capital and human capital. The movement toward greater use of physical capital had lost its significance by the 1973 sample break, however. The trends in the factor content of manufacturing imports were much the opposite, although there was no tendency in the physical capital coefficient. In particular, there was weak evidence of a declining human capital intensity in imports, but there were quite pronounced indications of a rising raw labor intensity. This is in accord with our previous finding that U.S. manufacturing imports have become more labor-intensive in the last two decades.

Results of Modified CUSUM Tests

We apply the modified CUSUM and CUSUM of SQUARES tests, developed in appendix A, to the pooled transformed data set, again employing net exports, exports, and imports as the dependent variables.

Tables 3.6 through 3.8 present the basic results of several modified CUSUM experiments, using industry net exports, exports, and imports, respectively, as the dependent variable. In the first of each pair of experiments we gave equal weights to each of the residuals resulting from the annual recursions, and in the second weights were assigned according to each industry's proportion of total real shipments. For purposes of discussion, denote these schemes as E and S, respectively. The dates listed in the tables are the years, if any, in which the CUSUM or CUSUM of SQUARES paths achieved the indicated significance levels.

Table 3.6. Results of Modified CUSUM and CUSUM of SQUARES Tests: Dependent Variable Net Exports

Technique	Recursion	Experiment	.10	.05	.01
CUSUM	Forward	E	1972	1973	1976
CUSUM	Forward	S	1963	1964	....
CUSUM	Backward	E	1966	1965	1962
CUSUM	Backward	S	1966	1965	1961
CUSUMSQ	Forward	E	1965	1967	....
CUSUMSQ	Forward	S	....	....	....
CUSUMSQ	Backward	E	....	....	....
CUSUMSQ	Backward	S	....	....	....

It is clear from table 3.6 that the modified CUSUM statistic was capable of illuminating evidence of structural change in the regression relationship under consideration. The forward recursion of the E path exhibited a steady downward drift, indicative of a tendency to overpredict net exports by industry, apparently beginning in the late 1960s. The cumulative effects of these

Table 3.7.   Results of Modified CUSUM and CUSUM of SQUARES
Tests: Dependent Variable Exports

Technique	Recursion	Experiment	.10	.05	.01
CUSUM	Forward	E	....	....	....
CUSUM	Forward	S	....	....	....
CUSUM	Backward	E	....	....	....
CUSUM	Backward	S	1967	1966	1963
CUSUMSQ	Forward	E	1965	1966	1967
CUSUMSQ	Forward	S	1965	1966	1967
CUSUMSQ	Backward	E	1972	1972	....
CUSUMSQ	Backward	S	....	....	....

Table 3.8.   Results of Modified CUSUM and CUSUM of SQUARES
Tests: Dependent Variable Imports

Technique	Recursion	Experiment	.10	.05	.01
CUSUM	Forward	E	1973	1974	1976
CUSUM	Forward	S	1963	1965	....
CUSUM	Backward	E	1967	1965	1962
CUSUM	Backward	S	1967	1965	1962
CUSUMSQ	Forward	E	1965	1966	1967
CUSUMSQ	Forward	S	....	....	....
CUSUMSQ	Backward	E	....	....	....
CUSUMSQ	Backward	S	....	....	....

overpredictions reached significance (10% level) in 1972. There was no reversal of this trend by the end of the period. With regard to the S scheme, however, there was a very early trend in the direction of underprediction, although this was reversed in the mid-1960s and there were no further indications of instability.[6]

The E and S experiments agreed in the backward recursions. In both cases there was a trend toward underprediction which attained significance in the latter part of the period. Both the forward and backward recursions exhibited long lags between the apparent beginning of the structural change and the attainment of statistical significance, which attests somewhat to the likely gradual nature of the shifts involved.

The last four lines of table 3.6 present the results of forward and backward recursions of the modified CUSUM of SQUARES statistics. Here the evidence of structural change was weaker, registering only in the forward E scheme. This change was experienced predominantly in the late 1960s.

Some indications of shifts in the structure of the exports equation appear in table 3.7. The CUSUM statistic gave little evidence of structural change in the exports relationship, with only the backward scheme achieving significance by virtue of a systematic tendency to underpredict the dependent variable. It should be pointed out that the forward E experiment was quite stable until the 1970s, during which time the path diverged sharply upward from the zero line, although failing to attain significance. The CUSUM of SQUARES tests, on the other hand, gave more pronounced evidence of structural change. Again, judging from the dates in the table, it would seem that the observed shifts predominantly transpired in the latter half of the period.[7]

Finally, with respect to the imports regression, there was again evidence of time-related structural change. In table 3.8 the E scheme tended toward underprediction, apparently beginning in the mid-1960s, and achieved significance in the early 1970s. The S scheme displayed early instability but reversed itself after 1965. The results of the backward recursions were virtually identical, with both the E and S schemes gradually moving toward larger cumulative overpredictions. The foreward E CUSUM of SQUARES also attests to the presence of shifts in the direct factor content of U.S. manufacturing imports, especially in the mid-1960s to early 1970s.

Our results thus far may briefly be summarized as follows. In the annual scaled regressions we found that the three-direct-factor-input model of U.S. manufacturing net exports was largely supported. There were indications of a declining raw labor coefficient and a rising human capital coefficient. Much the same may be said about exports separately. The three-direct-factor-input model also explains a significant portion of the variation in yearly imports. There was, as perhaps may have been expected, an increasing tendency over the period for manufacturing imports to make direct use of unskilled labor.

More striking evidence of structural change emerged from the tests on the pooled sub-samples which were detailed in table 3.5. In addition to reaffirming the results mentioned in the previous paragraph, the pooled analysis detected an increase in the physical capital intensity of exports and a decline in the human capital intensity of imports.

Finally, the CUSUM techniques were meaningfully extended to the pooled cross-section and time-series context by considering for each period the vector of prediction residuals which results from incorporating all the cross-section observations from that period. The modified CUSUM procedures were capable of unearthing evidence of structural change in the direct factor content of U.S. manufacturing net exports, exports, and imports. In particular, the recursive estimates of the regression coefficients tended to overpredict net exports by industry toward the end of the period. This is perhaps not surprising in light of the generally negative trend in industry trade balances which was highlighted in chapter 1.

Additional Perspective: Ricardo Goods and Technology-Intensive Goods

To complete this part of chapter 3 we now disaggregate the collection of manufacturing industries somewhat by considering two industry subsets. The first of these is the group of Ricardo goods as defined by Hufbauer and Chilas (1974). These goods are generally characterized by a relatively high natural resource content.[8] We separate this group for analysis because of the well-recognized special role that natural-resource industries seem to play in the determination of the factor content of manufacturing trade. The second is the set of technology-intensive goods (hereafter called TECH) as identified by Gruber, Mehta, and Vernon (1967). Separate analyses are performed for each of the two groups in order to ease to some extent the equality restrictions which we have placed on the regression coefficients across industries.

In the interests of brevity, we only verbally describe the results of the annual scaled regressions. For the Ricardo goods, the three-direct-factor model did not perform well in the net exports regressions, with only isolated coefficients achieving significance. However, when considered separately, both imports and exports of the Ricardo manufacturing industries were characterized by the use of physical capital throughout the period, with the import coefficients being generally higher than the export coefficients. These findings may reflect the supposed complementarity between physical capital and natural resource inputs in the production of such goods, whether produced at home or abroad. Interestingly, U.S. exports of manufactured Ricardo goods were characterized by a negative and generally significant relationship to human capital.

With regard to the TECH goods, there was a positive and highly significant relationship between net exports and human capital.[9] The relationship between net exports and physical capital was consistently positive, although generally insignificant, while net exports of TECH goods also tended to make relatively little use of unskilled labor throughout the period. TECH exports were characterized by the intensive use of both physical and human capital, but depended negatively on raw labor. Finally, the imports equation registered few coefficients which were significantly different from zero, although the relationship between TECH imports and raw labor was consistently positive, while that between TECH imports and human capital was consistently negative.

Tables 3.9 and 3.10 present the results of the simple tests for changes in the pooled coefficient regimes for the Ricardo and TECH goods.[10] The minima of the likelihood ratios for the first group occurred at 1971 (NX and M) and 1969 (X). From table 3.9 we see that, although the Ricardo net exports equation was apparently stable over the period, this was not true of the exports and imports equations. Apparently, the physical capital intensity of both manufactured

Table 3.9. Tests for Coefficient Changes among Pooled Sub-Samples: Ricardo Goods

Eq. No.	T	TC	L	K	H	DUMTC	DUML	DUMK	DUMH	R^2	F	F^1 in λ
Dependent Variable Net Exports												
(3.21)	..	$-.025$ $(3.57)^5$	.309 $(2.35)^4$	$-.053$ $(7.81)^5$	.009 (1.34)	....	....	....	....	.20	37.7^5	....
(3.22)	68	$-.031$ $(3.63)^5$	.449 $(2.79)^5$	$-.062$ $(7.06)^5$	.010 (1.05)	.020 (1.23)	$-.425$ (0.99)	.019 (1.28)	$-.005$ (0.35)	.21	19.6^5	1.5 / $-$ 11.1
(3.23)	71	$-.027$ $(3.45)^5$	.421 $(2.84)^5$	$-.056$ $(6.96)^5$	.005 (0.60)	.009 (0.43)	$-.198$ (0.34)	.011 (0.70)	.004 (0.23)	.20	10.3^5	0.9 / $-$ 15.9
Dependent Variable Exports												
(3.24)	..	.037 $(7.96)^5$	$-.492$ $(4.96)^5$	.085 $(17.54)^5$	$-.019$ $(3.79)^5$	....	....	....	....	.52	163.0^5	....
(3.25)	69	.034 $(6.71)^5$	$-.132$ (1.14)	.070 $(11.93)^5$	$-.031$ $(4.78)^5$	.003 (0.31)	.123 (0.38)	.053 $(5.23)^5$	$-.003$ (0.25)	.57	98.4^5	16.8^5 / $-$ 153.8
(3.26)	73	.038 $(8.05)^5$	$-.265$ $(2.49)^4$	.083 $(16.36)^5$	$-.032$ $(5.50)^5$	$-.004$ (0.25)	.850 (1.58)	.053 $(3.48)^5$	$-.006$ (0.39)	.55	93.2^5	11.8^5 / $-$ 73.1
Dependent Variable Imports												
(3.27)	..	.051 $(9.59)^5$	$-.559$ $(4.94)^5$	.115 $(19.77)^5$	$-.029$ $(5.90)^5$	....	....	....	....	.58	210.7^5	....
(3.28)	68	.050 $(7.91)^5$	$-.368$ $(2.72)^5$	.104 $(13.90)^5$	$-.035$ $(5.45)^5$	$-.011$ (0.88)	.379 (0.99)	.034 $(2.75)^5$	$-.002$ (0.17)	.59	110.0^5	4.5^5 / $-$ 14.8
(3.29)	71	.049 $(8.65)^5$	$-.410$ $(3.31)^5$	.106 $(15.61)^5$	$-.033$ $(5.86)^5$	$-.011$ (0.68)	1.20 $(2.22)^4$	.047 $(3.49)^5$	$-.019$ (1.28)	.60	112.6^5	6.7^5 / $-$ 19.6

3 = significant at the .10 level; 4 = significant at the .05 level; 5 = significant at the .01 level.

Table 3.10. Tests for Coefficient Changes among Pooled Sub-Samples: TECH Goods

Eq. No.	t	TC	L	K	H	DUMTC	DUML	DUMK	DUMH	R^2	F	F^1 ln λ
						Dependent Variable Net Exports						
(3.30)	..	-.027 (2.41)[4]	-1.63 (5.92)[5]	.132 (7.10)[5]	.045 (5.58)[5]	....	....	....	....	.20	43.3[5]	....
(3.31)	68	.016 (1.29)	-1.14 (3.17)[5]	.089 (4.16)[5]	.029 (2.70)[5]	-.174 (5.64)[5]	-1.80 (1.85)[3]	.162 (3.88)[5]	.071 (3.96)[5]	.25	29.2[5]	12.3[5] / -75.0
(3.32)	73	-.015 (1.30)	-1.54 (4.80)[5]	.122 (6.20)[5]	.041 (4.33)[5]	-.135 (2.86)[5]	-3.22 (1.50)	.088 (1.54)	.077 (2.74)[5]	.22	24.0[5]	4.0[5] / -8.6
						Dependent Variable Exports						
(3.33)	..	.046 (10.25)[5]	-1.33 (11.72)[5]	.076 (11.11)[5]	.036 (10.73)[5]	....	....	....	....	.74	496.2[5]	....
(3.34)	61	.049 (6.41)[5]	-.784 (3.65)[5]	.068 (5.79)[5]	.022 (3.07)[5]	.010 (1.07)	-1.52 (5.38)[5]	.000 (0.04)	.026 (3.15)[5]	.76	267.8[5]	11.0[5] / -26.5
(3.35)	73	.046 (10.04)[5]	-1.08 (8.14)[5]	.077 (10.66)[5]	.028 (6.96)[5]	.022 (1.09)	-1.87 (2.21)[4]	-.023 (1.07)	.029 (2.66)[5]	.75	254.5[5]	4.1[5] / -8.5
						Dependent Variable Imports						
(3.36)	..	.087 (11.20)[5]	.552 (3.07)[5]	-.044 (3.97)[5]	-.018 (3.28)[5]	....	....	....	....	.30	75.9[5]	....
(3.37)	68	.061 (6.96)[5]	1.06 (4.17)[5]	-.012 (0.97)	-.036 (4.31)[5]	.083 (4.09)[5]	.958 (1.42)	-.096 (4.06)[5]	-.007 (0.62)	.38	53.7[5]	22.3[5] / -77.4
(3.38)	73	.083 (10.35)[5]	1.00 (4.72)[5]	-.035 (3.08)[5]	-.033 (4.89)[5]	.067 (2.20)[4]	4.07 (2.72)[5]	-.075 (2.22)[4]	-.039 (2.17)[4]	.36	48.6[5]	15.3[5] / -31.4

3 = significant at the .10 level; 4 = significant at the .05 level; 5 = significant at the .01 level.

Ricardo exports and imports rose during the period, as did the unskilled labor intensity of imports.

The TECH likelihood ratios reached their lowest points at 1968 (NX and M) and 1961 (X). Again, the trends in these pooled coefficients are evident from table 3.10. The imports equation exhibited the most instability and was characterized by a rising dependence on raw labor and a declining dependence on physical capital and on human capital. TECH net exports and exports exhibited the opposite behavior, registering increases in human capital intensity and declines in labor intensity.

The results of applying the CUSUM procedures to the TECH net exports equation are summarized in table 3.11. As with the experiments presented earlier which incorporated all 120 industries, we find that the CUSUM procedures detected evidence of structural change more readily than the CUSUM of SQUARES techniques. Both the forward E and S schemes led to continuously growing cumulative overpredictions of TECH net exports, with the E scheme being perhaps the more powerful. The backward schemes also suggested changes in the regression relationship, with the recursive estimates tending toward ever larger underpredictions of the dependent variable. The S path actually went outside the upper 10% confidence limit in 1973, fell back within the confidence band, then continually diverged away from the zero line, beginning in 1970 and achieving significance in the mid-1960s.

Table 3.11. Results of Modified CUSUM and CUSUM of SQUARES Tests: TECH Goods Dependent Variable Net Exports

Technique	Recursion	Experiment	.10	.05	.01
CUSUM	Forward	E	1972	1972	1976
CUSUM	Forward	S	1972	1976	....
CUSUM	Backward	E	1962	1961	1958
CUSUM	Backward	S	1973, 1968	1965	1960
CUSUMSQ	Forward	E	1965	1968	....
CUSUMSQ	Forward	S	....	....	....
CUSUMSQ	Backward	E	....	....	....
CUSUMSQ	Backward	S	....	....	....

Before reporting the results of estimation and hypothesis testing in the next set of models, it is useful to review the findings to this point. It is clear that the direct factor content characteristics of U.S. manufacturing net exports, exports, and imports have undergone significant change in the period since 1958. The modified CUSUM tests, which provide only information on whether the overall regression relationships have changed, but which are most appropriate for this purpose in the present research, provided ample evidence on this point. Moreover, with few exceptions, it seems that these factor content changes have occurred as gradual trends, beginning in the early to mid-1960s and at times becoming more concentrated in the 1970s.

We have had to rely on dummy variable tests, both among the annual cross-sections and among pooled data sub-samples, to identify trends in the individual factor coefficients. Based on these results, it appears that U.S. net exports of manufactures have become progressively less unskilled labor-intensive and more human capital-intensive over the period. These conclusions were supplemented by the finding that the trends in the direct factor content of exports were similar to those of net exports, while the trends in the direct factor content of imports were of the opposite nature. The general picture, then, is one in which the domestic production of goods in which imports are relatively high made progressively greater use of raw labor and less use of skilled labor. The opposite was true with regard to the production of goods which are associated with relatively high exports. U.S. comparative disadvantage became increasingly characterized by unskilled labor inputs and U.S. comparative advantage became steadily more associated with the input of high labor skills.

We next compared the industry characteristics of Ricardo, or natural resource-intensive industries, and high technology industries. Not surprisingly, both exports and imports of Ricardo goods were characterized by a positive dependence on physical capital.[11] At the same time, the capital variable was significantly negative in the net exports equation as U.S. foreign trade served to economize on scarce natural resources, and hence on the complementary factor, capital. The equation was apparently stable, however. TECH net exports, on the other hand, became more human capital-intensive over the course of the period. That is, those high technology goods which are generally thought to represent the strongest area of U.S. comparative advantage in manufactures relied to an increasing extent on labor skills to maintain high levels of net exports.

Analysis of the Technological Content of U.S. Foreign Trade

In this section we incorporate variables which are commonly considered to be useful proxies for technological innovativeness. For this purpose, we constructed two measures of technological inputs by industry. The first is real research and development (RD) expenditures and the second is the number of full-time-equivalent scientists and engineers engaged in research and development (ES). Both of these variables were then scaled by the real value of shipments so as to represent "technological intensities" and to be consistent with our earlier models. The data for the technological inputs are available for 21 manufacturing industries at approximately the 2-digit SIC level on an annual basis for the period under consideration. Consequently, their inclusion in the analysis necessitated a certain amount of aggregation across industries of the trade and direct factor inputs variables.[12]

Tables 3.12–3.14 list the results of annual cross-section regressions of the three models over the aggregated data samples in selected years. The scaling of all variables is identical to that of the earlier models. The first regression for each year repeats our three-direct-factor-input models to determine how severely aggregation affects the results. With regard to the net exports equations (table 3.12), we find that the structure of the three-factor models remains largely unchanged. In all four years the human capital coefficients were positive and highly significant, the unskilled labor coefficients were negative and significant, while the physical capital variable was negative but generally insignificant. Notice also that the labor coefficient again fell over the period, while the human capital coefficient exhibited a slight upward trend.[13] Hence, our basic conclusions about the direct factor content characteristics of U.S. comparative advantage remain unchanged.

The situation with regard to manufacturing exports was similar (table 3.13). Again, a large and statistically significant proportion of the variation in the dependent variable was explained by the contributions of the three aggregated industry inputs. The raw labor coefficient declined significantly over the period, while the human capital intensity of exports rose. In addition, the physical capital intensity of exports declined markedly during the 1970s.

Finally, it seems that aggregation adversely affected the explanatory power of the imports equations (table 3.14). In no case was the regression relationship significant, and only the human capital variable registered coefficients which differed from zero. Notice that the signs of the L and H coefficients reversed in the 1970s. None of the coefficient changes was significant, however.

The remaining equations in tables 3.12–3.14 incorporate the technological variables separately. The most striking aspect of these regressions is the consistent decline in the t-statistics of the earlier inputs. This may be taken as evidence of multicollinearity among the variables of the expanded regressions. To get some perspective on this, we present in table 3.15 the simple correlation matrix among the independent variables at 1967, the middle year of the sample period. H and L are highly correlated, as would be expected from the construction of H. Notice the high correlations between H and the technological variables, however. Given these relationships, it becomes difficult for the regression procedure to identify the separate contributions of the skilled labor and technology inputs to the determination of net exports, exports, and imports.[14] RD and ES are almost perfectly correlated, so there is no reason to carry both of them along in the subsequent analysis. A glance at tables 3.12–3.14 confirms that, except for the magnitudes of the coefficients of

Table 3.12. Scaled Regressions for Aggregated Industry Cross-Sections, Selected Years Dependent Variable Net Exports (N = 21)

Year	C	L	K	H	RD	ES	R^2	F
1960	-.009 (0.31)	-1.28 (2.43)[4]	-.017 (0.56)	.065 (4.47)[5]	....	....	.55	6.92[5]
1960	.004 (0.13)	-1.05 (1.91)[3]	-.014 (0.48)	.043 (1.89)[3]	.216 (1.30)	....	.59	5.83[5]
1960	.000 (0.00)	-.970 (1.78)[3]	-.011 (0.37)	.038 (1.73)	....	12.33 (1.56)	.61	6.23[5]
1965	-.029 (0.87)	-1.45 (2.04)[3]	-.019 (0.46)	.074 (4.22)[5]	....	....	.53	6.49[5]
1965	-.029 (0.84)	-1.45 (1.77)[3]	-.019 (0.45)	.075 (2.76)[4]	-.004 (0.03)	....	.53	4.58[4]
1965	-.027 (0.34)	-1.33 (1.60)	-.016 (0.39)	.068 (2.36)[4]	....	2.84 (0.29)	.54	4.63[4]
1970	-.045 (1.03)	-2.05 (1.98)[3]	-.027 (0.58)	.087 (3.88)[5]	....	....	.48	5.21[5]
1970	-.050 (1.13)	-1.45 (1.15)	-.010 (0.20)	.065 (1.95)[3]	.296 (0.87)	....	.50	4.04[4]
1970	-.052 (1.18)	-1.27 (1.02)	-.003 (0.07)	.057 (1.67)	....	18.09 (1.14)	.52	4.30[4]
1975	-.024 (0.50)	-3.36 (2.06)[3]	-.111 (2.21)[4]	.099 (4.04)[5]	....	....	.51	6.01[5]
1975	-.056 (1.33)	-.763 (0.46)	-.042 (0.85)	.042 (1.47)	1.29 (2.80)[4]	....	.67	8.29[5]
1975	-.055 (1.28)	-.925 (0.56)	-.037 (0.72)	.040 (1.32)	.....	57.82 (2.68)[4]	.67	7.95[5]

3 = significant at the .10 level; 4 = significant at the .05 level;
5 = significant at the .01 level.

these variables, their effects on the regression relationships are virtually identical. In the remaining analysis, therefore, we include only the engineers and scientists variable as a proxy for technological innovativeness. This choice is made for two reasons. First, the use of ES avoids the problem of having to choose a suitable price deflator for the research and development variable. Second, since ES is measured in terms of number of employees, it is more akin to the stock concepts we have employed in measuring the other factor inputs. RD on the other hand, represents a flow per unit of time and is perhaps a less appropriate proxy for the stock of industry high technology.

We have mentioned the multicollinearity problems encountered in the annual cross-section regressions. The standard remedy for such a problem is to increase sample size either by expanding the cross-section coverage or by pooling cross-section and time-series data (Kmenta, 1971, p. 391). The much

Table 3.13. Scaled Regressions for Aggregated Industry Cross-Sections, Selected Years Dependent Variable Exports (N = 21)

Year	C	L	K	H	RD	ES	R^2	F
1960	.036 (1.49)	-1.07 $(2.53)^4$	$-.008$ (0.33)	.047 $(4.04)^5$	....	....	.49	5.49^5
1960	.049 $(1.98)^3$	$-.842$ $(1.97)^3$	$-.005$ (0.23)	.025 (1.45)	.205 (1.59)	....	.56	5.13^5
1960	.043 $(1.76)^3$	$-.845$ $(1.91)^3$	$-.004$ (0.15)	.028 (1.56)	....	8.63 (1.36)	.55	4.79^5
1965	.017 (0.64)	-1.03 $(1.81)^3$	$-.007$ (0.22)	.054 $(3.80)^5$	....	....	.48	5.28^5
1965	.017 (0.62)	-1.03 (1.55)	$-.007$ (0.21)	.054 $(2.46)^4$	.003 (0.02)	....	.48	3.73^4
1965	.018 (0.64)	$-.984$ (1.47)	$-.006$ (0.18)	.051 $(2.21)^4$	....	1.17 (0.15)	.48	3.74^4
1970	.030 (0.93)	-1.60 $(2.09)^3$	$-.027$ (0.78)	.066 $(3.99)^5$	....	....	.49	5.52^5
1970	.027 (0.82)	-1.22 (1.31)	$-.016$ (0.43)	.052 $(2.10)^3$	.186 (0.74)	....	.51	4.17^4
1970	.027 (0.82)	-1.23 (1.32)	$-.016$ (0.41)	.052 $(2.01)^3$	....	8.48 (0.71)	.51	4.14^4
1975	.061 (1.67)	-3.67 $(2.94)^5$	$-.125$ $(3.22)^5$	.098 $(5.21)^5$	....	....	.64	10.18^5
1975	.036 (1.13)	-1.58 (1.27)	$-.069$ $(1.86)^3$	.053 $(2.43)^4$	1.03 $(3.01)^5$	....	.77	13.51^5
1975	.038 (1.16)	-1.81 (1.42)	$-.068$ (1.72)	.053 $(2.27)^4$	....	44.02 $(2.66)^4$	.75	12.11^5

3 = significant at the .10 level; 4 = significant at the .05 level;
5 = significant at the .01 level.

greater amount of information should improve the precision of the estimates, and allow for the estimation of the separate contributions of the independent variables.

Before considering the pooled analysis of the expanded models, we consider the effects of aggregation on the stability of the pooled regression coefficients of the three-factor model. As may be seen in table 3.16, there were still indications of unstable coefficients between pooled sub-samples. In particular, when the sample was split at 1970 the labor coefficient declined significantly while the human capital intensity of net exports rose.[15] These results are consistent with those of table 3.5. Notice, however, that the physical capital coefficient declined rather markedly, implying a reduction in the direct capital content of manufactured net exports coming predominantly in the 1970s. These findings, along with the significance of the F^1 statistics in the final

Table 3.14.   Scaled Regressions for Aggregated Industry Cross-Sections, Selected Years Dependent Variable Imports (N = 21)

Year	C	L	K	H	RD	ES	R^2	F
1960	.045 (2.36)[4]	.192 (0.59)	.009 (0.48)	− .017 (1.88)[3]	....	....	.21	1.53
1960	.044 (2.13)[4]	.179 (0.50)	.009 (0.45)	− .016 (1.07)	− .011 (0.11)	....	.21	1.08
1960	.042 (2.14)[4]	.102 (0.28)	.007 (0.37)	− .009 (0.63)	....	− 3.51 (0.68)	.23	1.23
1965	.044 (2.41)[4]	.371 (0.94)	.011 (0.47)	− .018 (1.84)[3]	....	....	.18	1.26
1965	.044 (2.32)[4]	.379 (0.82)	.011 (0.45)	− .019 (1.22)	.004 (0.04)	....	.18	0.89
1965	.043 (2.28)[4]	.300 (0.64)	.009 (0.39)	− .014 (0.92)	....	− 1.15 (0.22)	.21	1.04
1970	.072 (2.74)[4]	.380 (0.63)	.000 (0.00)	− .018 (1.32)	....	....	.10	0.62
1970	.074 (2.72)[4]	.182 (0.24)	− .006 (0.19)	− .010 (0.51)	− .102 (0.49)	....	.11	0.50
1970	.075 (2.82)[4]	.004 (0.01)	− .011 (0.38)	− .003 (0.15)	....	− 8.87 (0.92)	.14	0.67
1975	.082 (3.17)[5]	− .433 (0.50)	− .021 (0.76)	.005 (0.37)	....	....	.04	0.22
1975	.087 (3.19)[5]	− .835 (0.78)	− .031 (0.98)	.014 (0.73)	− .199 (0.67)	....	.06	0.28
1975	.087 (3.23)[5]	− .885 (0.84)	− .034 (1.06)	.016 (0.82)	....	− 10.72 (0.79)	.07	0.32

3 = significant at the .10 level; 4 = significant at the .05 level; 5 = significant at the .01 level.

column, suggest that aggregation across industries did not serve to eliminate the instability in the coefficient regimes which we have observed.

Table 3.17 presents the results for the expanded models. It is clear from equations (3.42), (3.45), and (3.48) that pooling reduced the severity of the multicollinearity. The net exports equation performed as expected, with U.S. comparative advantage over the period being marked by the intensive use of human capital and high technology inputs, and comparative disadvantage being associated with the use of unskilled labor and physical capital. That is, both neo-factor proportions and neo-technology elements have been important. Similar comments apply to the exports equation. The inclusion of ES changes the signs of the coefficients of the imports equations relative to what they had been in earlier experiments, however. In particular, the production of imports in the expanded model seems to have been characterized by a negative relationship with unskilled labor and a somewhat positive

Table 3.15.   Correlation Matrix of Scaled Independent Variables, 1967
(N = 21)

Variable	L	K	H	RD	ES
L	1.000				
K	-.299	1.00			
H	.661***	-.170	1.000		
RD	.136	-.217	.635***	1.000	
ES	.170	-.238	.657***	.969***	1.000

*** = significant at the .01 level.

relationship with human capital. These results are puzzling in light of the scaling we have chosen.[16] Perhaps expectedly, technological inputs do not characterize the production of import-competing manufactures.

The inclusion of the technology variable generally tended to reduce, but not eliminate, the instability in the pooled regression relationships as a comparison of the ln λ and F^1 columns in tables 3.5 and 3.17 indicates. The likelihood ratio of the net exports equation reached its minimum at 1970. Curiously, the ES variable exhibited the only significant change, with the technology intensity of net exports rising over the period. The inclusion of this variable eliminated the instability previously noted in the pooled L and H coefficients.[17] Again, similar comments apply to the exports equations.

The likelihood ratio of the imports equation reached its minimum in 1967. The anomalous results of equation (3.48) were somewhat intensified as U.S. manufacturing imports became less labor-intensive and more human capital-intensive in the 1970s, according to this model.

Finally, we present the results of the CUSUM tests on the extended models in tables 3.18 through 3.20. The net exports equation showed pronounced signs of structural change when the technology variable was included, as may be seen from table 3.18. Both the forward E and S schemes exhibited a gradual tendency to overpredict the vector of net exports, beginning in the early to mid-1960s and achieving statistical significance in the early 1970s. The backward schemes were consistent with these findings, continually tending toward larger cumulative underpredictions which went outside the significance bands by the end of the experiment. Again, these trends may be taken as evidence of gradual, continual structural change spread out fairly evenly over the period. The CUSUM of SQUARES tests gave somewhat less marked indications of instability, as might be expected, but again pointed to the mid-1960s as the time period in which the changes may have been most concentrated.

Table 3.16. Tests for Coefficient Changes in the Three-Factor Model among Pooled Sub-Samples of the Aggregated Data Set: Dependent Variable Net Exports

Eq. No.	t	TC	L	K	H	DUMTC	DUML	DUMK	DUMH	R^2	F	$F^{[1]}$ ln λ
(3.39)	..	-.045 (4.69)[5]	-.687 (3.84)[5]	-.023 (2.31)[4]	.061 (14.59)[5]	....	....	....	....	.42	88.6[5]	....
(3.40)	67	-.039 (2.87)[5]	-1.02 (3.74)[5]	-.001 (0.05)	.065 (10.03)[5]	.011 (0.55)	-.477 (1.06)	-.069 (3.46)[5]	.009 (1.04)	.47	51.8[5]	8.4[5] - 28.5
(3.41)	70	-.043 (3.69)[5]	-.982 (4.12)[5]	-.003 (0.21)	.065 (11.29)[5]	.015 (0.79)	-1.09 (2.04)[4]	-.089 (4.29)[5]	.020 (2.11)[4]	.48	52.4[5]	11.1[5] - 33.7

3 = significant at the .10 level; 4 = significant at the .05 level; 5 = significant at the .01 level.

Table 3.17. Tests for Coefficient Changes among Pooled Sub-Samples of the Aggregated Data Set

Eq. No.	t	TC	L	K	H	ES	DUMTC	DUML	DUMK	DUMH	DUMES	R^2	F	F[1] ln λ
					Dependent Variable Net Exports									
(3.42)	..	-.018 (2.13)[4]	-.800 (4.72)[5]	-.024 (2.52)[4]	.040 (8.18)[5]	15.34 (6.45)[5]	....	....	....	....	....	.46	81.1[5]	....
(3.43)	70	-.022 (2.11)[4]	-.921 (4.05)[5]	-.009 (0.80)	.050 (6.25)[5]	6.71 (2.25)[4]	-.008 (0.50)	-.275 (0.54)	-.039 (0.47)	-.005 (0.47)	32.51 (5.46)[5]	.54	53.5[5]	14.8[5] -35.3
(3.44)	73	-.023 (2.55)[4]	-.877 (4.42)[5]	-.014 (1.35)	.047 (7.15)[5]	9.54 (3.60)[5]	-.013 (0.62)	-.202 (0.25)	-.035 (1.24)	-.010 (0.68)	47.48 (5.20)[5]	.53	52.4[5]	10.6[5] -24.7
					Dependent Variable Exports									
(3.45)	..	.040 (6.87)[5]	-1.07 (10.47)[5]	-.028 (4.08)[5]	.043 (12.33)[5]	10.92 (6.08)[5]	....	....	....	....	....	.56	385.0[5]	....
(3.46)	70	.035 (5.28)[5]	-.796 (6.18)[5]	-.011 (1.50)	.035 (6.77)[5]	6.88 (3.19)[5]	-.011 (1.00)	-.125 (0.45)	-.025 (1.88)[3]	.006 (0.74)	34.10 (7.88)[5]	.67	265.1[5]	29.1[5] -61.6
(3.47)	73	.034 (5.80)[5]	-.891 (7.96)[5]	-.014 (2.14)[4]	.039 (9.00)[5]	8.11 (4.30)[5]	-.013 (0.99)	.347 (0.78)	-.022 (1.24)	-.008 (0.85)	53.55 (8.42)[5]	.67	263.7[5]	25.1[5] -44.2
					Dependent Variable Imports									
(3.48)	..	.062 (12.77)[5]	-.430 (5.10)[5]	-.008 (1.57)	.009 (3.19)[5]	-8.84 (6.10)[5]	....	....	....	....	....	.32	263.7[5]	....
(3.49)	67	.049 (6.94)[5]	.015 (0.12)	.004 (0.60)	-.007 (1.36)	-3.70 (1.72)[3]	.020 (2.00)[4]	-.390 (1.82)[3]	-.016 (1.44)	.015 (2.26)[4]	-4.71 (1.37)	.37	143.5[5]	6.15[5] -17.2
(3.50)	73	.057 (10.40)[5]	-.193 (1.93)[3]	-.001 (0.09)	.000 (0.02)	-6.17 (3.64)[5]	.017 (1.36)	.123 (0.31)	-.015 (0.96)	.003 (0.32)	3.03 (0.52)	.37	141.9[5]	5.4[5] -9.8

3 = significant at the .10 level; 4 = significant at the .05 level; 5 = significant at the .01 level.

Table 3.18. Results of Modified CUSUM and CUSUM of SQUARES
Tests on Aggregated Data Set: Dependent Variable Net Exports

Technique	Recursion	Experiment	.10	.05	.01
CUSUM	Forward	E	1972	1973	1976
CUSUM	Forward	S	1973	1975	....
CUSUM	Backward	E	1960	1958	....
CUSUM	Backward	S	1963	1962	1958
CUSUMSQ	Forward	E	1965	....	....
CUSUMSQ	Forward	S	1965	1967	....
CUSUMSQ	Backward	E	1967	1966	....
CUSUMSQ	Backward	S	....	....	....

Table 3.19. Results of Modified CUSUM and CUSUM of SQUARES
Tests on Aggregated Data Set: Dependent Variable Exports

Technique	Recursion	Experiment	.10	.05	.01
CUSUM	Forward	E	....	....	....
CUSUM	Forward	S	....	....	....
CUSUM	Backward	E	1966	1964	....
CUSUM	Backward	S	....	....	....
CUSUMSQ	Forward	E	1968	1969	....
CUSUMSQ	Forward	S	....	....	....
CUSUMSQ	Backward	E	....	....	....
CUSUMSQ	Backward	S	....	....	....

Table 3.20. Results of Modified CUSUM and CUSUM of SQUARES
Tests on Aggregated Data Set: Dependent Variable Imports

Technique	Recursion	Experiment	.10	.05	.01
CUSUM	Forward	E	1973	1974	1976
CUSUM	Forward	S	....	....	....
CUSUM	Backward	E	1966	1965	1962
CUSUM	Backward	S	1965	1965	1962
CUSUMSQ	Forward	E	1964	1965	1967
CUSUMSQ	Forward	S	1965	1965	1967
CUSUMSQ	Backward	E	....	....	....
CUSUMSQ	Backward	S	....	....	....

The exports experiments (table 3.19) indicated relative stability, with only the backward E CUSUM and forward E CUSUM of SQUARES tests registering significant changes in the coefficient regimes.

It is clear from table 3.20 that the coefficients of the imports equation in the aggregated data set were relatively unstable. The forward E CUSUM test led to cumulatively larger underpredictions of the vector of industry imports by the technology variable-inclusive model, which reached significance by the end of the period. The backward CUSUM experiments were similarly unstable. Finally, the forward CUSUM of SQUARES experiments concurred in their assessment of the existence and timing of the structural shifts involved, although corroboration from the backward tests was not registered.

To summarize this final section of the econometric analysis, three points may be made. First, the technological input variables we have chosen are somewhat collinear with some of the other factor inputs, and consquently statistical inference in the annual cross-section models was rendered rather difficult to make. As a result, pooled analysis became even more desirable than before. Second, the simple pooled tests for structural change (table 3.17) seemed to suggest that the inclusion of the technology variable was sufficient to eliminate practically all of the instability previously noted in the labor, physical capital, and human capital coefficients of the various models. The technology variable itself exhibited instability, with both manufacturing net exports and exports becoming significantly more intensive in the use of RD scientists and engineers over the period. There apparently was no noticeable change in the tendency of imports to be characterized by a relative lack of use of the same variable. Third, the CUSUM tests confirmed the existence of structural change in the extended models, although the relative lack of evidence on this score in the exports equation suggests that the strong results of equations (3.43) and (3.44) in table 3.16 may have been overstated.

4

Interpretation of Results and Implications for Future Research

In this chapter we discuss developments in the factors which may underlie the changes we have observed in the characteristics of U.S. manufacturing foreign trade. The chapter consists of five sections. In the first section we recount our major findings. In the middle three sections we focus on the three underlying trade determinants which shall be suggested as possible factors contributing to the observed shifts. These are trends in relative factor endowments, major changes in commercial and tax policies, and technological progress. The final section summarizes the research and comments on possible implications for future analysis.

Review of Findings and General Comments

We have thus far been concerned with determining whether and how the characteristics of U.S. comparative advantage, as measured by scaled net exports, have changed over the period in question. We have also been interested in changes in the characteristics of exports and imports separately. We have accomplished these ends by comparing the magnitudes of the coefficients in annual cross-section regressions and in pooled regressions. In addition, use was made of modified forms of the CUSUM and CUSUM of SQUARES tests since these latter procedures should be fairly sensitive to gradual or unconcentrated structural change. Our major findings were as follows:

1. In the annual scaled regressions we found that the three-direct-factor model of U.S. manufacturing net exports was largely supported. Comparing the annual regressions over time, it was found that U.S. comparative advantage moved increasingly away from raw labor (or, perhaps stated more appropriately, comparative disadvantage came to be increasingly marked by the use of unskilled labor) while the human capital intensity of net exports rose slightly. The comparisons

of the pooled sub-samples confirmed these findings, and suggested that the decline in the raw labor content of manufacturing net exports was more concentrated after 1969.

2. Similar comments apply to the coefficients of the exports equations. In addition, there was some indication in the pooled analysis of a rise in the physical capital intensity of manufacturing exports.

3. There were pronounced suggestions of a rising raw labor intensity of manufactured imports, both in the annual comparisons and the pooled comparisons. There may also have been a decline in the human capital intensity of imports.

4. The modified CUSUM experiments yielded further evidence of changes over time in the coefficients of the three-direct-factor-input model of U.S. net exports, exports, and imports. The Quandt and CUSUM tests suggested that in nearly all cases the coefficient regime changes were characterized by gradual shifts over time as the cumulative underpredictions or overpredictions of the vectors of the dependent variables slowly achieved significance.[1] Further, in many instances it seemed likely that the indicated structural change had its genesis several years prior to the point of significant departure from the mean value line under the null hypothesis. This points to the existence of rather steady change over time, quite often beginning in the mid-to-late 1960s.

5. We next examined the performance of the three-factor models in two industry sub-groups. Ricardo goods or natural-resource-intensive goods comprised the first sub-group. The most striking result here was the positive and significant relationship between physical capital inputs on the one hand and Ricardo exports and imports on the other hand. This was taken to reflect the supposed complementarity between physical capital and natural resource inputs in the production of such goods, a notion which has often been cited as a contributing factor to the Leontief paradox since this relationship was believed to be more important on the imports side. Indeed, the capital coefficients of both the Ricardo exports and imports pooled equations rose significantly over the period, although the increase in the exports equation coefficient was proportionately higher than the increase in its imports equation counterpart. This convergence of manufactured natural-resource-intensive exports and imports in their capital requirements, in conjunction with the decline in the relative importance of Ricardo goods in U.S. trade noted in chapter 1, serves to help explain the apparent reversal of the paradox by the early 1970s. The second sub-group was composed of high technology goods, referred to here as TECH goods. TECH net exports registered

significant increases in human capital intensity and declines in raw labor intensity. This instability was again confirmed by the modified CUSUM tests.

6. Finally, we examined trends in the technology content of U.S. foreign trade in manufactures by incorporating a proxy for high technology inputs into the various models. Doing so required a large amount of aggregation across industries, reducing the number of cross-sectional units available for analysis from 120 to 21. It appeared from this analysis that U.S. comparative advantage came to be marked increasingly by the intensive use of advanced technology, as evidenced by significant increases in the engineers and scientists coefficient in the net exports equation over time. The same result was observable in the exports equation.

We have thus documented in detail the kinds of shifts in the characteristics of U.S. manufacturing trade which have transpired, according to our data, in the last two decades. In each of the next three sections we describe, in turn, how changes in certain underlying trade determinants may influence our coefficient estimates. Available information is then examined to assess how important the influences may have been.

Changes in Relative Factor Endowments

By the logic of the neo-factor proportions theory, changes in relative factor endowments among trading partners will affect the commodity composition and factor content of trade. As Stern (1975, pp. 18–19) points out:

Thus, the structure and factor content of trade will change over time, especially in response to differential rates in the accumulation of physical and human capital. International labor migration and direct foreign investment will also affect factor endowments and trade.... A more complete understanding of the evolution of the structure and factor content of trade thus requires explicit recognition of differential factor accumulation and international factor movements.

Hence, any test for changes in the structure of U.S. trade should be coupled with an examination of trends in relative factor endowments among the U.S. and its trading partners.

An increase in the U.S. relative abundance of human capital, for example, will, ceteris paribus, render the human capital-intensive sectors even more advantaged in international trade compared with other sectors. By our interpretation of the regression coefficients as outlined in chapter 2, we would expect such a development to be reflected in an increase in the human capital coefficient of the net exports equations and perhaps a decline in the other coefficients as well. The impact on the exports and imports equations coefficients is more difficult to ascertain since these variables are not really accurate reflections of comparative advantage or disadvantage. However, other things equal, an increase in the human capital coefficient of the exports equations should be consistent with a rise in the relative human capital endowment of the U.S. since this would tend to reduce the relative price and thereby raise the exports of human capital-intensive goods which, as we have seen, form the primary basis of U.S. export strength. At the same time, an increase in the American human capital endowment might be expected to reduce imports of human capital services as goods which are relatively intensive in this factor but produced elsewhere come to be more disadvantaged. On this score we might expect a falling sign on H in the imports equations to be consistent with a rise in U.S. human capital abundance relative to the rest of the world. More generally we would expect, ceteris paribus, that the direction of the change in the factor intensity coefficients would correspond positively with the change in a particular relative factor endowment in the net exports and exports equations, yet negatively in the imports equations.[2]

With these comments in mind, consider our basic results. U.S. comparative advantage in manufactured goods seems to have been marked by a rise in the use of human capital services and a decline in the use of unskilled labor services. In addition, there was perhaps a reduction in the physical capital content of manufacturing net exports, although in general the relationship between U.S. comparative advantage and this factor remains fairly ambiguous as the exchange of physical capital services through exports and imports has been relatively balanced. These findings would be consistent with an increase in the U.S. comparative abundance of human capital and/or an increase in the relative labor scarcity of this country.

Bowen (1980b) provided information on the U.S. share of the world supply of skilled and semiskilled labor, unskilled labor, and physical capital in the years 1963 and 1975. According to his figures, the U.S. share of the world capital stock fell from 41.9 percent to 33.4 percent between those years, while its share of human capital fell from 29.4 percent to 26.3 percent, and its share of unskilled labor fell from 0.6 percent to 0.2 percent. In addition, the U.S. share of semiskilled labor rose slightly over the period. As a result, the U.S. has become increasingly abundant in skilled and semiskilled labor relative to capital and unskilled labor.[3]

Consider our three factors in turn. Skilled labor is often equated with human capital as a factor of production and so we shall attempt to compare Bowen's findings on skilled labor with our results on human capital.[4] Bowen reported that the U.S. annual growth rate of skilled labor per worker between 1963 and 1975 was sufficiently slow at 1.27 percent that the U.S. fell from a rank of second highest endowment of skilled labor per worker to seventh highest. By 1975 it ranked behind Sweden, Israel, Norway, Netherlands,

Finland, and France, all of which may be classified as developed countries (DCs) except perhaps Israel. The U.S. maintained a substantial, if slightly narrowed, advantage on this score relative to the group of less developed countries (LDCs) examined. These developments were reflected in a decline in the 1970s in the ratio of skilled to total labor services embodied in U.S. manufacturing exports to the DCs and a steady rise in this ratio in manufacturing exports to the LDCs.[5] Comparing these findings with our results for the full data sample (table 3.5) and for the set of technology-intensive goods (table 3.10), it seems justifiable to claim that the significant increases in the human capital content of U.S. manufactured net exports and exports may well be due to the continued abundance in the U.S. of human capital relative to the LDCs, combined with a shift in the composition of manufacturing trade toward the LDCs.[6] American comparative advantage continues to lie substantially in the realm of goods which are intensive in human capital, and this is true despite the slight deterioration in the U.S. share of world skilled labor relative to some other DCs.

As we have stated, our results with regard to the physical capital input were mixed. Based on the disaggregated data set regressions listed in table 3.5, it would seem that net exports relied negatively on the input of capital, although the relationship was positive for imports and exports (the regression counterpart of the Leontief paradox). Yet there were apparently no changes in these relationships, except for a slight increase in the capital intensity of exports, as a glance at the dummy coefficients suggests. The situation was somewhat different when we considered Ricardo and TECH goods separately (tables 3.9 and 3.10). We have already discussed the probable nature of the rising capital coefficients in the Ricardo imports and exports equations, in terms of capital-natural resource complementarity, while no changes were indicated in the net exports equation. TECH goods, on the other hand, registered a marked increase in the capital content of net exports and a decline in the capital content of imports. These findings might suggest that the relative U.S. physical capital endowment has gone up over the period, as Stern and Maskus (1981) reported.[7] On the other hand, when we considered the three-direct-factor-input model in the aggregated data set (table 3.16) we found a reduction in the physical capital content of overall manufactured net exports. This result is in fact consistent with Bowen's findings of a marked decrease in the U.S. relative endowment of capital. The rate of growth of capital per worker between 1963 and 1975 was 1.7 percent, causing the U.S. to drop from first to sixth in the world on a capital per worker basis.

Finally, with very few exceptions, our empirical analysis indicated a declining unskilled labor intensity of U.S. manufacturing net exports and exports, and a rising unskilled labor intensity of imports. These results accord with the previously reported decline in the U.S. share of the world endowment of raw labor.

To summarize, our results are broadly consistent with the available information on changes in U.S. relative endowments of unskilled labor, physical capital, and human capital. It has long been recognized that differential rates of factor accumulation due to population growth, investment, and factor migrations exert a powerful influence on the structure of world trade. It has not been possible here to assess objectively the effects that factor accumulation alone has had on our regression coefficients. Yet the large amount of evidence we have presented with regard to the instability of the coefficients, combined with our understanding of the pace and direction of changes in relative factor endowments, leads us to conclude that endowment changes have in fact significantly influenced the characteristics of U.S. foreign trade in manufactures.

Commercial Policy Changes

It has long been recognized that government commercial policies, here taken to include tariff and nontariff barriers (NTBs) together with relevant domestic taxes, can influence the structure of a country's international trade. Travis (1972) claimed that the U.S. protective structure has sufficiently inhibited the international flow of factor services to distort the pattern of factor exchange we might expect on the basis of more traditional determinants of comparative advantage, such as factor endowments.[8] Consequently, negotiated reductions in tariff and nontariff barriers to trade may result in an increased rationalization of the factor content of trade over time. In addition, Melvin (1970) has argued that commodity taxation can be an independent trade determinant, with the pattern of trade depending on whether a production or consumption tax was levied. Melvin (1979) also presented evidence that the U.S. corporate income tax has disadvantaged American capital-intensive industries enough to offset the comparative advantage they may otherwise have had due to the relative abundance of capital in the U.S. We have also mentioned that Deardorff (1979) has shown in a two-factor model that the existence of tariffs and traded intermediate goods can upset any a priori rankings of comparative advantage by commodity.

This brief discussion points up the notion that commercial policies, by distorting relative domestic and international prices and hence causing resource misallocations, serve to disrupt the pattern of trade in commodities and in factor services which would occur in their absence, and which would be driven by elements such as factor proportions and technological innovativeness. It is, of course, very difficult to discern exactly what the effects are of the various policies, either separately or in combination. U.S. agricultural policy, for example, has long provided price supports for certain commodities which keep their domestic prices above world prices. At the same time, the U.S. government provides export subsidies for these same commodities so as to make their prices competitive in foreign trade. The net result, besides the artificially high prices to American consumers, is a set of agricultural commodities which are internationally competitive, a fact which probably would be true anyway in the absence of price supports and subsidies, given the structure of American resources (Baldwin, 1970). Further, it has never been very clear in an empirical sense what effects the world protective structure has had on the implicit exchange of factor services. Baldwin (1971) confirmed that U.S. tariffs and major NTBs have operated in the direction of the Leontief paradox (raising the capital-labor ratio in imports relative to that in exports) but doubted that removal of all American and foreign trade-distorting commercial policies would have reversed the paradox. From the standpoint of correlation or regression analysis, it is difficult to say with certainty how tariffs and the like will affect the factor content of trade. In general, however, these measures will restrict U.S. imports which, given the presumed nature of world resource endowments and technology, would tend to be labor-intensive on average. Further, high levels of protection are generally afforded to American labor-intensive goods (e.g., textiles, footwear) so that on this score the labor content of imports is reduced from what it would otherwise be. At least with regard to the U.S., trade in other manufacturing goods has been relatively unrestricted over the period.[9]

Again, the ideal procedure would be to find annual data at a disaggregated industry level for each of the many trade barriers and market distortions which might affect the pattern of trade, or at least construct some effective protection equivalent of the combined effects of these many elements, and include these observations in the regression analysis. We could thereby note the relationship, if any, between comparative advantage and the artificial trade impediments. Such a procedure is, of course, impossible and we are forced to consider our coefficient changes in light of what we know about commercial policy shifts. For example, a rising (falling) raw labor coefficient in the imports (exports or net exports) equation would here be taken to be consistent with a dismantling of trade resistance variables which served to restore somewhat the trade pattern we would observe based on traditional comparative advantage considerations.

We shall consider the effects of two broad policy actions. The first consists of the Kennedy Round of tariff negotiations held during the years 1962–1967.[10] The Kennedy Round negotiations were in fact the sixth post-war set of multilateral meetings held under the auspices of the General Agreement on Tariffs and Trade (GATT), although none of the earlier talks was very successful at meaningfully reducing trade barriers.[11] The Kennedy Round negotiations did not accomplish much in the way of reducing NTBs, although some agreement on antidumping practices was reached. The talks were far more successful in reducing tariff barriers on nonagricultural goods. In particular (Jackson, 1977, p. 479):

Tariff reductions of 50 percent were made on a broad range of nonagricultural products, and smaller, but significant, reductions on many more. It is estimated that (in terms of trade coverage) roughly two-thirds of the duty reductions made by participants negotiating on a linear, across-the-board basis (the United States, the European Economic Community, the United Kingdom, Austria, Denmark, Finland, Norway, Sweden, Switzerland, and Japan) were reductions of 50 percent or more. The United States made concessions of this magnitude on $6.4 billion of its imports in 1964.

Hence, tariff reductions among the DCs were clearly rather substantial. Also of interest were the tariff concessions with respect to the LDCs. The latter countries were permitted to participate in the negotiations without being required to make fully reciprocal tariff reductions and the U.S. granted most of its concessions to the group under the most favored nation (MFN) principle. Some efforts were also made to reduce import duties on products of particular interest to the LDCs. The net result was that the U.S. made concessions affecting over $900 million of the trade of the developing countries as of 1965.

It is difficult to assess the overall impacts of these concessions on the characteristics of U.S. manufacturing trade. On the one hand, one might argue that they benefited LDC exporters very little since the effective protection structure of the U.S. and the other DCs, along with many of the NTBs, remains biased against the manufactured exports in which the developing countries have an actual or potential interest in expanding. On the other hand, our results strongly indicate the rising (declining) unskilled labor content of U.S. manufactured imports (net exports and exports) which points to the opening up of U.S. markets to LDC producers.[12] Indeed, the Kennedy Round concessions were gradually phased in over a five-year period (1967–1972) which closely coincides with the timing and the pace of many of the structural changes we have observed in the current analysis. It seems reasonable to conclude on this basis that tariff reductions have played a role in the changing structure of U.S. trade, a role which would have been even larger had the negotiations been successful at reducing or eliminating the many nontariff barriers to trade. Further multilateral negotiations should seek to reduce as many of these barriers as possible, thereby fostering additional specialization and trade along the lines of true comparative advantage.

The second set of policy actions concerns provisions of U.S. tax law which apparently have acted to restrict domestic investment. In the previous section we traced the movements in relative factor endowments among the U.S. and its trading partners. We noted the relatively slow rate of physical capital accumulation in the U.S. over the last two decades. This low rate of investment has been a major force behind relative U.S. declines in productivity growth. To some extent this undoubtedly reflects the simple shifting of comparative advantage as other countries have caught up with and even surpassed the huge absolute advantage in this factor which the U.S. enjoyed in the post-war period. However, some observers point to U.S. tax law as a major underlying cause of reduced domestic investment.[13] We have already mentioned that there is some evidence that the U.S. corporate income tax acts to restrict the export of U.S. capital services relative to what it would be on the basis of simple factor endowments. In addition, U.S. and foreign tax laws often provide a strong incentive for U.S. based multinationals to invest in facilities overseas. Both the foreign tax credit (which allows a firm to take as a credit against its U.S. tax liability the amount of taxes paid to other governments) and the deferral of tax on foreign subsidiary income (which provides that income earned by foreign subsidiaries of U.S. firms is not taxed unless that income is repatriated) have been cited as inducements for American firms to divert their investment plans overseas.[14] The ability to engage in transfer pricing also has encouraged the establishment of some overseas operations. This way the firm can place its profits at the stage of production which lies in the country with the most favorable tax laws. Partly as a result of all this, the rate of growth of sales by foreign subsidiaries of U.S. manufacturing firms has outpaced the rate of growth of U.S. exports of manufactured goods, at least until the 1970s. The ratio of the sales of foreign affiliates to U.S. exports of manufactured goods rose from 1.6 in 1959 to 2.4 in 1976, down from a peak of 2.7 in 1973.[15]

In summary, our results seem to be consistent first with the general liberalization of world trading practices under the GATT, and especially the opening up of U.S. and other DC markets to the manufactured exports of LDCs. The result has been a restructuring of trade patterns along the more traditional lines of comparative advantage. Hence, any further efforts at reducing tariff and nontariff barriers so as to encourage additional rationalization of trade and to increase the real income gains therefrom, should meet with success. On the other hand, it appears that U.S. tax law has had a hand in diverting capital resources away from domestic investment, thereby restricting American productivity and growth relative to what it might otherwise have been.[16] Both of these trends are of a long-term structural nature, and help to explain the secular changes in the characteristics of U.S. manufacturing trade which we have observed.

Technological Progress

It is difficult rigorously to predict the effects which various types of technical change may have had on our regression coefficients. On the one hand, labor-augmenting technical change, for example, should reduce the amount of labor needed to produce a given amount of output and (making the appropriate demand assumptions) net exports so that on this account we might expect the raw labor coefficients in our comparative advantage models to fall over time, as they have. On the other hand, this labor-augmenting technical progress may be viewed as an increase in the effective supply of American labor, implying an increase in the U.S. relative unskilled labor endowment. Thus, what matters is what happens to factor endowments and the resulting technological coefficients when all output responses have been worked out. In this regard, it seems that factor-augmenting progress, by raising the relative supply of a factor and thereby reducing its relative autarky price, should raise the implicit intensity of that factor in net exports. Consequently, we make no claims about the expected changes in the regression coefficients given certain types of technical progress. It seems clear, however, that technological advance had some effects on the coefficients of the three-factor models, for recall that much of the instability in these coefficients was eliminated when we incorporated a proxy for technological innovativeness. It would seem that the three-factor models thus suffered from a misspecification.[17]

We may perhaps gain a better understanding of the effects of technological change if we consider them in the context of dynamic comparative advantage. In particular, the product cycle model is essentially a model of innovation, direct foreign investment, and changing factor mix over the life of the cycle. It is clear from our results on the technology content of trade that U.S. manufacturing comparative advantage continues to lie, and even has a growing stake, in high-technology goods. Such products generally are at or near the beginning of the cycle, that is, the innovation stage in which a new product or process is introduced. The production of a new good is characterized by the intensive use of skilled labor and technological inputs since its production process is relatively unstable, requiring frequent adjustments in design and implementation. In particular (Hirsch, 1967, p. 19), "... new products contain a high proportion of scientific and engineering inputs." Since the product is new, the innovating country has a monopolistic advantage in its production and export, if such markets exist. The advantage is only temporary, however. After some time, the product enters the "growth" stage in which production volume expands quickly and becomes more physical capital-intensive, although skilled labor remains an important input. In this stage the U.S. may well maintain its comparative advantage, given its relatively abundant supplies of physical and human capital. On the other hand, production of this good may shift in this stage to other relatively capital-abundant countries as American firms attempt to exploit foreign markets by actions other than exporting, such as licensing or investing in subsidiaries. Hence, in this growth stage, investment may naturally be diverted overseas.

After another period of time, the product becomes "mature." Production of the good achieves standardization and the factor mix changes from being primarily skilled labor and physical capital-intensive to being primarily physical capital and unskilled labor-intensive. Clearly, the LDCs will have a comparative advantage in the production of mature goods. Indeed, the U.S. is quite likely to find itself importing the good which it originally innovated after enough time has elapsed so that production of the good becomes standardized and hence cheaper in other countries.

Our empirical results would suggest that U.S. net exports and exports have remained intensive in their content of skilled labor and advanced technology. This is evidence that, on average, U.S. manufactured exports lie in those sectors which are in the new or growth stages. In fact, this has apparently been a rising trend. Manufactured imports, on the other hand, tend to make relatively little use of human capital and advanced technological inputs. Hence, to the extent that the product cycle model presents a valid picture of the determinants of manufacturing trade, it seems that, on average, U.S. imports are in the mature phase of the cycle. The picture which emerges is one in which the U.S. has been able to maintain, and perhaps even expand, its temporary monopoly advantages in the technology-intensive trade which has been the mainstay of its export strength in manufacturing, by continually innovating and introducing new products. Yet enough time has passed that an increasing range of goods which used to represent areas of American export strength (communications equipment, televisions, and the like) are now in the mature phase and hence produced and exported by relatively labor-abundant areas. The net result has been a continued and rising dependence of U.S. comparative advantage on skilled labor and research and development, combined with a growing dependence of manufactured imports on raw labor.

Conclusions and Implications for Future Research

With this research we have presented detailed evidence with regard to long-term structural changes in the characteristics of U.S. manufacturing trade. This was accomplished by applying extensions of several structural change techniques to a large, disaggregated, pooled cross-section and time-series data set covering the factor intensity characteristics of nearly all U.S. manufacturing industries. In addition, we examined the technological characteristics of trade by examining a series of extended models in a more aggregated set of data.

Generally speaking, we have found that the intensive use of unskilled labor has increasingly come to characterize those industries in which the U.S. is at a comparative disadvantage. At the same time, U.S. comparative advantage has been marked by a growing relationship with human capital and advanced technology. The industries which intensively use these latter inputs have, of course, represented the strongest areas of American competitive export strength in the last several decades.

We have made an effort to identify movements in the underlying determinants of the structure of trade which could explain the shifts we have discovered in the characteristics of manufacturing trade. To a great extent, our observations undoubtedly reflect natural developments in the structure of world comparative advantage. The United States emerged from World War II with its capital base intact and a relatively abundant supply of human capital. Consequently, it found itself with a huge absolute and comparative advantage in the production of all types of manufactured goods, including consumer goods. During the 1950s and 1960s, however, the locus of physical capital abundance shifted somewhat away from the U.S. and toward the rapidly growing set of competitor countries, most notably Japan, the European Economic Community, and the Scandinavian countries. Relative factor endowments are likely to continue changing in a direction which will remove additional manufactured goods from the range of American comparative advantage. The so-called newly industrializing countries, such as Korea, Mexico, and Argentina, are accumulating larger shares of the world supplies of physical capital and semiskilled and skilled labor.

We have also argued that recent changes in commercial policy in the U.S. and elsewhere may have contributed to the increasing rationalization of world and U.S. manufacturing trade. It is hoped that the narrow protectionist interests which appear to be emerging will not reverse the gains experienced from the Kennedy Round and those yet to be realized from the Tokyo Round of multilateral tariff negotiations.

Finally, we should point out that, although it is clear that the best U.S. prospects for continued export growth lie in the human capital and advanced technology-intensive industries, it is not clear that this country will be able to maintain its strong trade position with respect to these goods. We have noted the relative decline in the skilled labor endowment of the U.S. At the same time, the research and development effort in the U.S. has lagged behind that of its chief competitors in the last fifteen years or so. For example, total U.S. research and development expenditures as a percentage of Gross National Product declined from 2.98 percent in 1965 to 2.38 percent in 1975.[18] In addition, much of the U.S. research and development effort has been aimed at national defense and space exploration; relatively little has been devoted to economic development and basic science. On all these fronts, the U.S. has been surpassed by a number of competitor developed countries. If we are to maintain or expand U.S. export strength in the future, some policy actions must be directed to the increased accumulation of human capital along with a more favorable environment for conducting research and development.

With regard to future research, the following seem to be areas most in need of further analysis:

1. We have made numerous allusions to the possibility that some of our results may at least partially derive from differences in the characteristics of U.S. trade with the developed versus the developing countries. Disaggregating the trade statistics on this basis (or perhaps even a finer division of country groups) would provide valuable information in this respect.

2. It might also be instructive further to disaggregate the set of industries beyond the Ricardo, TECH, and other industries division which we have employed.

3. The biggest shortcoming of the present analysis was its inability to quantify the impacts the various trade determinants (factor endowments, commercial policies, and technological progress) may have had on the regression coefficients. To do so would necessitate the assembly of a massive new set of data, and the development of techniques for analyzing the contributions of these factors to the various coefficient changes. It is difficult to see how this might be done, but, if possible, such an analysis would be of great help to researchers and policymakers in their future ruminations about changes in the determinants of the structure of U.S. foreign manufacturing trade.

Appendix A

Econometric Methodology

This appendix presents, in general terms, the techniques to be used for the analysis of structural change in the various regression specifications. The first section formally sets out the nature of the econometric hypotheses with which we shall be concerned. The second section briefly reviews simple techniques which are to be employed in checking for constancy across the separate annual cross-section regressions. The final three sections deal with procedures which are relevant for the analysis of coefficient stability in the pooled cross-section and time-series context.

Statement of Hypotheses

Consider the question of testing for structural change in a pooled cross-section and time-series model:[1]

$$Y_{it} = x'_{it}\beta_t + \epsilon_{it} \quad i = 1, 2, \ldots, N, t = 1, 2, \ldots, T \quad (A.1)$$

where at time t and for cross-sectional unit i, Y_{it} is the observation on the dependent variable and x_{it} is the column vector of observations on K regressors. We advance the following maintained hypothesis:

(MH.1) all regressors are non-stochastic, or, if stochastic, independent of the error terms;

(MH.2) the error terms ϵ_{it} are normally and independently distributed with means zero and variances σ_t^2, $t = 1, \ldots, T$;

(MH.3) parameters may vary only over time, so that variation among cross-sectional units is ruled out.

The reasoning behind these assumptions is as follows. Assumption (MH.1) is standard and should pose no particular problem here. It will be maintained throughout the analysis. We adopt (MH.2) in this appendix strictly for purposes of exposition, since the procedures to be outlined below rely on such an assumption. Notice that the assumed error structure precludes the possibilities of autocorrelation and heteroskedasticity within the pooled data set. Since these problems are likely to exist in any practical application, however, a discussion of transformations which are designed to correct for them is included at the end of this appendix. Of course, this recognition of the problems of serial correlation and heteroskedasticity removes (MH.2) from the maintained hypothesis which we specify with respect to the original data set and places it into the maintained hypothesis which is relevant for the transformed set of observations.

Finally, assumption (MH.3) imposes constancy across the cross-sections. That is, it is assumed here that no change in the parameters occurs compositionally across industries while time-related change is allowed. We listed our reasons for making this assumption in chapter 2.

Consequently, the testable hypotheses are

$$H_0: \quad \beta_1 = \beta_2 = \ldots = \beta_T = \beta \tag{A.2}$$
$$\sigma_1^2 = \sigma_2^2 = \ldots = \sigma_T^2 = \sigma^2.$$

H_A: not H_0.

We shall be more concerned with detecting differences among the β's than among the σ^2's, so that explicit tests for variation in the latter group of parameters are not given here.

Tests for Comparisons among Cross-Sections

The first step in the empirical analysis will be to run separate annual cross-section regressions over the period in question. This exercise will provide evidence on the direct factor content of manufacturing trade in each year.

Of interest here is the issue of changes over time in the regression coefficients. A simple dummy variable specification will suffice to check for significant differences in these coefficients between pairs of years. The technique, which is taken from Kmenta (1971), is outlined in the next few sentences.

Consider a regression, assuming, without loss of generality, that there are two explanatory variables in addition to the constant term, in which we pool the observations from two separate years, t_0 and t_1, in the following manner:

$$Y = \beta_0 + \beta_1 X_1 + \beta_2 X_2 + \gamma_0 Z + \gamma_1 Z X_1 + \gamma_2 Z X_2 + \epsilon , \tag{A.3}$$

where $Z = 0$ if $t = t_0$ and $Z = 1$ if $t = t_1$, and the cross-section and time-series subscripts, i and t, have been suppressed. It is clear that in order to check for significant changes in the coefficients between years t_0 and t_1 we need only examine the individual null hypotheses which are implicit in

$$H_0: \quad \gamma_0 = \gamma_1 = \gamma_2 = 0. \tag{A.4}$$

A t-test on the estimated γ coefficients will suffice for this task.

In addition, we may consider (A.4) as an hypothesis with regard to significant variation in the overall regression relationship. In this case, we simply run regressions on the two cross-sections separately and also on the pooled cross-sections, and then employ an appropriate F-test which considers the significance of the reduction of the sums of squared errors which results from removing the equality constraints on the estimated coefficients (Kmenta, 1971).

Simple Tests for Coefficient Constancy in the Pooled Context

One of this study's contributions is to perform a pooled analysis of the question of shifts over time in the factor content of trade. The rationale for pooling is quite simple. By combining cross-sectional data over a lengthy period, the researcher is able to improve the precision of his/her coefficient estimates by virtue of the much larger number of degrees of freedom. In addition, confident resolution of the kinds of questions being posed here requires a large amount of information over a sustained time period. Finally, the results from a pooled analysis will be relevant for examining the robustness of the evidence from other more restricted tests for changes in the structure of trade (Aho and Carney, 1979).

As a beginning in this regard, suppose there may exist two separate parameter regimes. The hypotheses to be considered are

$$H_0: \quad \beta_1 = \beta_2. \tag{A.5}$$

$$H_A: \quad \text{not } H_0.$$

We seek an approach which will provide information on the existence, timing, and sharpness of any changes experienced. Further, we would like to have some knowledge of which parameters may have individually undergone structural variation, rather than testing strictly for joint variation.

With regard to the timing of any regime change, Quandt (1958) suggests examining the log-likelihood of the sample, assuming normal disturbances which are independent both of each other and of the explanatory variables, in an effort to find the true change point.[2] In general form, the log-likelihood is

$$L(y, t^*) = -(NT/2)\ln 2\pi - (Nt^*/2)\ln \sigma_1^2 - (N\{ T - t^*\}/2)\ln \sigma_2^2$$

$$- 1/2\sigma_1^2 \sum_{1}^{N} \sum_{1}^{t^*} (y_{it} - x'_{it}\beta_1)^2 - 1/2 \sigma_2^2 \sum_{1}^{N} \sum_{t+1}^{T} (y_{it} - x'_{it}\beta_2)^2. \quad (A.6)$$

The objective is to find maximum likelihood estimates of

β_1, β_2, σ_1^2, σ_2^2 and t^*.

Conditional on t^*, the MLE's of β_1 and β_2 will be identical to ordinary least squares estimates derived from running regressions on the first Nt^* and the last $N(T - t^*)$ observations, respectively. In addition, MLEs of σ_1^2 and σ_2^2 are straightforward. The procedure, then, is to calculate for each possible t^* the values

b_1, b_2, $\hat{\sigma}_1^{\,2}$, and $\hat{\sigma}_2^{\,2}$.

Substitute these into (A.6) and choose as the MLE for t^* that $\hat{t}^*$ which makes (A.6) the largest.

Estimation of $\hat{t}^*$ provides some information on the timing of the switch. In addition, a plot of the ratio of the log-likelihood under H_0 and that under H_A against time will yield some crude knowledge of how gradual or abrupt the change has been. A jagged minimum at $\hat{t}^*$ indicates abrupt change, while a smoother plot is indicative of gradual shifts. [3]

By way of corroboration of the results of the foregoing techniques, two other procedures will be employed. First, F-tests will be performed to test for the equality of two pooled regressions, breaking the sample at arbitrary points in time, such as at mid-sample (1968) or at the $\hat{t}^*$ indicated by the Quandt procedure. [4] Second, dummy variables will be constructed to examine changes over time in the individual regression coefficients from the pooled analysis. These latter tests are clearly analogous to those mentioned in the previous section, with appropriate adjustments for the number of degrees of freedom.

The conclusions of all these simple procedures will be subject to at least one important caveat, however. To apply effectively these sample splitting techniques, we must believe that the switching point was rather abrupt and that the imposed split is near the actual one. This latter point is important in order to avoid the possibility of excessive contamination of the estimates of one regime structure by data which were in fact generated by another regime. The verity of these beliefs is doubtful in the present context. It seems unlikely that changes in the dependence of trade performance over time on structural variables such as factor proportions could be concentrated at a single point in time. Rather, we would expect the types of adjustments considered here to take some time to work themselves out. Consequently, inferences from procedures which rely on the assumption of sharply defined separate parameter regimes are liable to be somewhat misleading. The next section considers some means for overcoming this difficulty.

Modified Cumulative Sums Tests

As a consequence of the caveat expressed at the end of the last section, we would like to adopt an approach which is more appropriate for the analysis of gradual or less concentrated structural change. One such procedure is comprised of the pair of techniques advanced by Brown and Durbin (1968) and Brown, Durbin, and Evans (1975). These are the cumulative sums (CUSUM) and cumulative sums of squares (CUSUM of SQUARES) tests based on the recursive residuals of successive least squares prediction. Consider for now the question of structural change in a single time-series. Under the null hypothesis of no change the residuals from successive predictions of the dependent variable, observation by observation, should not depart much from zero. However, if some change does occur then these residuals will diverge from zero in the post-change period. The same is true of standardized cumulative sums of these residuals and of standardized cumulative sums of squares of these residuals. By graphing these latter two statistics against time, and by placing critical bands around their expected-value lines under H_0, it is possible to test for significant change at various prescribed significance levels. If either path wanders outside the significance lines, there is evidence of structural change. Corroboration on this point is available from a backward recursion of the same relationships from the end of the period to the beginning.

Application of the CUSUM technique to our problem is desirable. By examining the cumulative sums of prediction errors after or even during the actual structural change, this approach will detect the aggregated effects of the shift, whether it is concentrated or gradual. Although it does not allow us to claim precisely what the timing of the change was, it often provides some useful bounds on this question.[5]

Although we have established the desirability of the CUSUM procedure, it cannot be applied in our pooled context without some modification. Recall the regression model

$$Y_{it} = x'_{it}\beta + \epsilon_{it} \tag{A.7}$$

is really a multiple equation specification in which we stack the cross-sections annually over the T periods. Consequently, the usual CUSUM procedure, which updates the regression with each successive observation, would simply add one industry at a time within each year until N, 2N, and so on observations have been included. Conceptually, then, the procedure would principally test for change among the cross-sections, rather than over time as we have specified. In addition, the length of the CUSUM plot would be tremendously long, realizing that N is 120 and T is 19.

Consider instead a modification in which the regression is updated annually by adding all N observations simultaneously. The result is a vector of N residuals at each step, and we would like to specify some meaningful summary statistic which incorporates information from all of them. The assumption again is that time-related influences tend to affect all industries uniformly. Consequently, if there has been some change, then this residual vector will diverge from the zero vector thereafter.

The problem may be formally stated as follows: let X_t^a denote the matrix of observations from period t on the N cross-sections, and let y_{it} denote the vector of observations on the dependent variable. Then, as a first step, estimate

$$y_1 = X_1^a \beta + \epsilon_1 \tag{A.8}$$

so that

$$b_1 = (X_1^{a\prime} X_1^a)^{-1} X_1^{a\prime} y_1.$$

Next we stack the N observations from the succeeding year to get

$$Y_2 = X_2 \beta + v_2 \tag{A.9}$$

where $\quad Y_2 = \begin{bmatrix} y_1 \\ y_2 \end{bmatrix}, \quad X_2 = \begin{bmatrix} X_1^a \\ X_2^a \end{bmatrix}, \quad v_2 = \begin{bmatrix} \epsilon_1 \\ \epsilon_2 \end{bmatrix}.$

Then, $b_2 = (X_2'X_2)^{-1}X_2'Y_2$, and, in general,

$$Y_t = X_t \beta + v_t, \text{ where } Y_t = (y_1, y_2, \ldots, y_t)',$$

$$X_t = \begin{bmatrix} X_1^a \\ X_2^a \\ \cdot \\ \cdot \\ \cdot \\ X_t^a \end{bmatrix}, \tag{A.10}$$

and $b_t = (X_t'X_t)^{-1}X_t'Y_t$.

Consider now the forecast error vector:

$$v_t = Y_t - X_t^a b_{t-1},$$ \hfill (A.11)

which is of dimension $(N \times 1)$.

Under H_0 we see that

$$E(v_t) = 0$$ \hfill (A.12)

and

$$V(v_t) = \sigma^2 \{X_t^a(X_{t-1}'(X_{t-1})^{-1}X_t^{a\prime} + I\} = \sigma^2 \Omega_t.$$

Further, by the normality of the error vector, we may say that

$$v_t \sim N(0, \sigma^2 \Omega_t).$$ \hfill (A.13)

Next we may compute the standardized mean forecast residual

$$v_t^* = \alpha' v_t / \sqrt{\alpha\ '\ \Omega_t\ \ \alpha\ \ },$$ \hfill (A.14)

where α is an $(N \times 1)$ vector of parameters which serve to weight the cross-section residuals, and recognize that

$$E(v_t^*) = 0$$ \hfill (A.15)

and

$$V(v_t^*) = \sigma^2\alpha,\quad \Omega_t/\alpha'\Omega_t = \sigma^2\ .$$

It is a straightforward matter to show that

$$E(v_t v_s') = \{0\}\ (t < s)$$

so that in view of their normality the forecast error vectors are independent, as are the standardized mean forecast residuals. Hence, if we consider the modified CUSUM statistic

$$W_t^* = 1/\hat\sigma \sum_2^t v_j^*,\quad t = 2,\dots,T$$ \hfill (A.16)

where $\hat{\sigma}$ is estimated from the full sample, then the sequence

$$W_2^*, W_3^*, \ldots, W_t^*$$

forms a sequence of approximately normal variables with the same general properties as the CUSUM sequence in Brown, Durbin, and Evans. In particular, $E(W_t^*) = 0$ so that we may place a pair of lines symmetrically above and below the zero line such that the probability that the modified CUSUM plot W_t^* crosses either is the desired level of significance. Appropriate critical values are given in the Brown, Durbin, and Evans paper.

Consider next the test which uses the squared recursive standardized mean forecast errors and is based on the plot of the modified CUSUM of SQUARES

$$s_t^* = \sum_2^t (v_j^*)^2 \Big/ \sum_2^T (v_j^*)^2, \qquad t = 2, \ldots, T \ . \tag{A.17}$$

This test is complementary to the modified CUSUM of SQUARES test and is especially helpful if changes in the β vector of regression coefficients are rather haphazard. Again, on H_0 this test statistic has the same general properties as those claimed for the CUSUM of SQUARES test in Brown, Durbin, and Evans and critical values for the location of the appropriate confidence bands around the mean value line

$$E(s_t^*) \;\; = \;\; (t - 1)/(T - 1)$$

may be found therein.

Some comments about these techniques are in order. The test statistics (A.16) and (A.17) are analogous to the CUSUM and CUSUM of SQUARES procedures themselves; however, the present statistics incorporate information from all cross-sections in each period by virtue of the averaging procedure chosen. An implicit weighting scheme is naturally included due to the use of the variance-covariance matrix. Notice also that we could allow for great generality in the averaging by an appropriate choice of the α parameter vector. For example, each residual could be weighted equally by using the vector of ones. More generally, we might use some vector of scalars which conveys information which is considered meaningful, such as each industry's proportion of the total manufacturing shipments or the like.

Problems with Pooling

Note that pooled regression analysis is complicated by the possibilities of heteroskedasticity within the annual cross-sections and serial correlation within each time-series. The presence of heteroskedasticity in the unadjusted data is to be expected in the present context, since, for example, trade balances will vary for no other reason than industry size. However, our models have been scaled for industry size which, as will be seen in chapter 3, is sufficient to remove the problem of heteroskedasticity in the annual cross-sections. Hence, no further adjustments are made on this account. At the same time, there may be good reason to suspect the presence of serially correlated disturbances in a trade relationship, since the effects of unobservable random factors in one period are likely to carry over to the following periods.

As a result, in each instance in which we pool the scaled data set, we first check each cross-sectional unit for the presence of first-order autocorrelation by means of the Durbin-Watson test. The resulting $\hat{\rho}_i$'s are then used to transform the data in the usual Cochrane-Orcutt fashion by industry, although a first period adjustment is included so as to maintain as many degrees of freedom as possible. The transformed NT disturbances which remain are then asymptotically $NID(0,\sigma^2)$. In other words, after the transformations we have NT observations on the well-behaved stacked model

$$y_{it}^* = x_{it}^{*\prime}\beta + \epsilon_{it}^* . \tag{A.18}$$

This is merely a simple application of generalized least squares. All pooled analyses will be performed on model (A.18).

Finally, it should be pointed out at this juncture that, as we have mentioned, data deficiencies force us to consider relatively simple models which accordingly may suffer from misspecifications. Indeed, any findings of structural change may themselves be the result of specification errors due to omitted variables. We will have more to say about this in chapter 4 and in appendix B.

Appendix B

Econometric Notes

In this appendix we explore the effects of excluding certain explanatory variables from the analysis, due to data deficiencies.

With regard to excluded explanatory variables, recall that a fully specified model of the determinants of trade would include productive factor intensities, high-technology intensity, scale economies, resistance variables, and domestic market distortions by industry (see equation (2.1)). In addition, we might wish to include a variable which somehow reflects consumer tastes. As we have mentioned, observations on many of these variables are unavailable on an annual basis at a disaggregated industry level. However, data do exist for a reasonable range of these variables (and industries) in the census years 1960 and 1970. We now incorporate several of these "excluded" variables and examine the possible implications of their exclusion for the biases of the "included" variables.

The problem may formally be stated as follows (Maddala, 1977, pp. 154–55):

Suppose the true model is

$$Y = X_1\beta_1 + X_2\beta_2 + \epsilon \qquad (B.1)$$

but we estimate

$$Y = X_1\beta_1 + V. \qquad (B.2)$$

Then we can show that

$$E(B_1) = \beta_1 + (X_1'X_1)^{-1}X_1'X_2 \qquad (B.3)$$

$$= P\beta_2$$

where B_1 is the OLS estimator of β_1. Notice that P is simply the matrix of coefficients which would result from a set of "auxiliary" regressions of each of the variables in X_2 on all the included variables. These regressions are auxiliary in the sense that X_1 and X_2 are nonstochastic so that the coefficients may be computed without variance. Thus, the biases of the estimated coefficients of the included variables depend on P and on the true coefficients of the excluded variables.[1] It should be noted that the estimated variances of the included coefficients are biased upward so that, in any case, the significance tests we have been using thus far have been conservative.

Four additional variables were chosen to incorporate into the analysis. The first was a measure of tariffs (calculated import duty as a percentage of import value) by industry to reflect the set of resistance variables. The final three were measures of scale economies, product differentiation, and the consumer goods ratio, adapted from Hufbauer (1970). Sample sizes are noted in the sequel.

Each part of the analysis proceeds in two steps. We first incorporate the additional variable(s) into the regressions and note the implications for coefficient stability. Second, we provide reasonable suppositions about the biases of the coefficients we have calculated in the body of the text. For brevity, we report only the results of the net exports equations; the results of the exports and imports equations are available upon request.

We consider two models. In the first, we incorporate the tariff measure to see how it singly affects the coefficient estimates. The results of this model were as follows (suppressing subscripts for notational ease and representing tariffs by T); recall that significance levels are represented as *(.10), **(.05), and ***(.01):

1960   (N = 58):   NX =   −.010   −.167L   +.001K   +.007H
                            (.064)   (0.99)   (0.80)   (0.95)

        +24.27ES   −.001T   +   e; R^2 =   .31, F =   4.60***
        (3.79)***   (1.04)

1970   (N = 73):   NX =   −.009   −.459L   +.049K   +.001H
                            (.050)   (2.90)*** (2.06)**   (0.15)

        +43.97ES   −.002T   +   e; R^2 =   .40, F =   9.00***
        (4.64)***   (1.55)

Pooled (N = 131):   NX =   −.012   −.294L   +.023K   +.006H
                            (1.07)   (3.19)*** (1.85)*   (1.96)*

        +32.06ES   −.001T   +   e; R^2 =   .33, F =   12.43***
        (5.86)***   (1.70)*

In the dummy-variable regression (not shown), there was weak evidence of an increase in the technology intensity of net exports between 1960 and 1970. No other coefficient changes were significant. Further, there was no significant change in the overall regression relationship. On the basis of this evidence it seems that a more fully specified model served further to reduce the variability in the coefficient estimates.[2]

When the remaining variables were included, the results became (letting S, G, and P represent scale economies, consumer goods ratio, and product differentiation, respectively):

1960	(N = 47):	NX =	−.018	−.189L	+.12K	+.008H
			(0.59)	(0.90)	(0.77)	(0.90)
	+24.30ES		−.007T	−.015S	−.008G	+.006P;
	(2.86)***		(0.63)	(0.07)	(0.21)	(0.17)
	R^2 = .33, F = 2.38**					

1970	(N = 62):	NX =	−.049	−.603L	+.060K	−.004H
			(1.53)	(3.41)***	(2.32)**	(0.70)
	+41.45ES		−.002T	−.179S	+.004G	+.072P;
	(3.42)***		(1.59)	(1.02)	(0.11)	(2.29)**
	R^2 = .50, F = 6.56***					

Pooled	(N = 109):	NX =	−.037	−.331L	+.024K	+.005H
			(1.66)	(3.21)***	(1.78)*	(1.44)
	+31.07ES		−.001T	−.106S	−.013G	+.043P;
	(4.45)***		(1.37)	(0.84)	(0.51)	(1.88)*
	R^2 = .38, F = 7.75***					

In the dummy-variable regression, there were no significant changes indicated in any of the coefficients. Neither was the change in the overall regression relationship significant. Hence, we might conclude that expanded models of the determinants of manufacturing net exports are subject to little, if any, structural instability. On the other hand, the evidence on which this statement is based derives from a more aggregative data set, incorporating far fewer years. The much greater amount of data involved in the calculations of chapter 3 lends those findings considerable credence. The truth is no doubt somewhere between the extremes; the case for structural shifts in the determinants of U.S. manufacturing trade was perhaps overstated in chapter 3, but on the other hand it was not misstated.

With regard to coefficient biases, we present in tables B.1 and B.2 the signs of the coefficients from the P matrix (see the earlier discussion) in the years 1960 and 1970, respectively. Each column represents the coefficients of a regression of the indicated variable on the X matrix.

Table B.1. P Matrix, 1960

XVAR	T	S	G	P
C	+	+	+	+
L	+	−	+	+
K	−	−	−	−
H	−	+	−	+
ES	−	+	−	+

There were only two sign changes, those on b_{sh} and b_{gh}.

Table B.2. P Matrix, 1970

XVAR	T	S	G	P
C	+	+	+	+
L	+	−	+	+
K	−	−	−	−
H	−	−	+	+
ES	−	+	−	+

Given these P matrices, we need to speculate about the signs of the true parameters in β_2. As is well known, tariffs may, in theory, impact either negatively or positively on net exports. There was very little significant evidence of any relationship on this score in the regressions presented earlier, although the sign on T was consistently negative in both years. Hence, we assume that the true sign on T is marginally negative, at best. The true coefficient on scale economies should theoretically be positive, while that on the consumer goods ratio should be negative. Finally, the true sign on the product differentiation variable is most likely positive for the U.S.

Combining these pieces of information, we present in table B.3 the expected direction of bias in the estimated coefficients of the included variables. As is no doubt always the case in a regression model with many excluded and included variables, it was in most cases impossible to predict the direction, much less the magnitude, of the coefficient biases. The exceptions were H in 1960 and ES in both years, the coefficients of which appear to have been biased upward. Indeed, many of the biases offset each other in direction so that the net effect on the final coefficient estimates may well have been rather small. We conclude, therefore, that the existence of coefficient biases due to excluded variables, though undoubtedly a problem, should not have affected our results or their interpretation to any substantial degree.

Table B.3. Expected Biases of Included Variable Coefficients

XVAR	1960	1970
C	?	?
L	?	?
K	?	?
H	+	?
ES	+	+

Appendix C

Data Sources and Construction

Data on the values of exports and imports by 3-digit SIC industry for 1958–1972 were obtained from the annual publications of the Bureau of the Census, *U.S. Commodity Exports and Imports as Related to Output*, and for 1973–1976 from the annual publications of the Bureau of the Census, *U.S. Exports/Domestic Merchandise, SIC-Based Products by World Areas*, Report FT 610, and *U.S. Imports/Consumption and General, SIC-Based Products by World Areas*, Report FT 210.

The classification of 3-digit SIC industries into Ricardo, Heckscher-Ohlin, and Product Cycle goods for the purpose of calculating the trade balances depicted in figure 1.1 was based upon Hufbauer and Chilas (1974, pp. 35–38), as follows:

Ricardo goods (N = 33): SIC 201–209; 211–213; 241–244; 249; 261–263; 266; 291; 295; 299; 311; 313; 324–325; 327–328; 333; 335–336.

Heckscher-Ohlin goods (N = 74): SIC 221–225; 227–229; 231–239; 251–254; 259; 264–265; 271–279; 284–285; 301–303; 306–307; 314–317; 319; 321–323; 326; 329; 331–332; 341–346; 348–349; 363; 365; 369; 371; 373–375; 379; 391; 393–396; 399.

Product Cycle goods (N = 28): SIC 281–283; 286–287; 289; 351–359; 361-362; 364; 366–367; 372; 381–387.

The industries which were eliminated from the analysis because of missing observations were 237; 251–254; 259; 274–279; 344; 359. This left 120 industries available for analysis.

For the division into Ricardo and TECH goods, we employed the Ricardo industries as listed, but a choice of TECH industries which differed from the Product Cycle list. TECH goods, taken from Gruber, Mehta, and Vernon (1967, p. 23), consisted of industries numbered 281–287; 289; 351–358; 361–367; 369; 371–375; 379; 381–387.

Data on employment and total payrolls by SIC industry were taken from various issues of the Bureau of the Census, *Annual Survey of Manufactures*. There was a substantial redefinition of SIC industries in 1972, details of which are available in the 1972 *Census of Manufactures*, Vol. 1. We attempted to maintain continuity in the industry definitions for the entire period, but some changes in coverage could not be satisfactorily resolved so that our results before and after 1972 may not be strictly comparable.

Data on the value of shipments by SIC industry for 1958–1971 were obtained from the annual publication, *U.S. Commodity Exports and Imports as Related to Output,* and for 1972–1976 from the *Annual Survey of Manufactures: Industry Profiles* (1976).

The capital-stock data by 3-digit SIC industry refer to gross stocks unadjusted for depreciation. The nominal and constant dollar (1958) capital stocks by industry for 1958–1971 were taken from U.S., General Services Administration, Office of Emergency Preparedness, *Capital Stocks Figures (Final), Input-Output Sectors, SIC Level with Vintage* (May, 1974). These data were extended to 1972–1976 using information on the book value of fixed assets by industry contained in the *Annual Survey of Manufactures: Industry Profiles* (1976). Some adjustments in industry coverage were required to obtain consistency over the entire period. All the capital-stock data were converted to constant (1967) dollars using implicit rebasing factors listed in the OEP source. In the absence of capital-stock deflators for 1972–1976, we imputed an annual increase in each industry's real gross fixed assets equal to a moving arithmetic average of the growth rates of these assets over the preceding four years. Details of these various adjustments and imputations are available upon request.

The values of exports, imports, and shipments were converted to constant (1967) dollars by means of price deflators constructed for each 3-digit SIC industry. These deflators were based upon data taken from various issues of U.S. Bureau of Labor Statistics, *Wholesale Prices and Price Indexes.* The particular wholesale price indexes chosen were concorded to an industry basis, using the value of industry shipments for individual years as noted in the sources mentioned above. Details of the concordance and weights used are available upon request.

To construct our measure of human capital, the wage of unskilled labor was taken as the median income of persons aged 25 and over of all races and both sexes, with eight or less years of schooling. This measure was constructed from various issues of the U.S. Bureau of the Census, *Current Population Report: Consumer Income,* Series P-60. For 1959, 1960, and 1962, when data were not available, the unskilled wage was interpolated linearly from the estimates constructed for adjacent years.

The estimates of human capital and the number of engineers and scientists for the 1960 and 1970 3-digit SIC industry cross-sections (see appendix B) were constructed from U.S. Bureau of the Census, *U.S. Census of Population: 1960, Final Report PC(2)-7A, Occupational Characteristics,* Table 32; *U.S. Census of Population: 1960, Occupation by Industry, Final Report PC(2)-7C,* Table 2; *U.S. Census of Population: 1970, Subject Reports, Final Report PC(2)-8B, Earnings by Occupation and Education;* and *U.S. Census of Population: 1970, Occupation by Industry, Final Report PC(2)-7C.* The estimates of research and development expenditures by industry for 1960 and 1970 were based upon National Science Foundation, *Research and Development in Industry, 1971.*

With regard to the observations in the aggregated data set, the figures on factor employments, shipments, and trade were simple aggregations across industries of the 3-digit SIC data. The annual observations on research and development expenditures and the number of scientists and engineers engaged in research and development were taken from various issues of National Science Foundation, *Research and Development in Industry.* The industry coverage, and thus the implicit aggregation scheme, included the following set of industries (N = 21): SIC 20; 22, 23; 24, 25; 26; 281, 282; 283; 284–289; 29; 30; 32; 331, 332; 333–336; 34; 35; 366–367; 361–365, 369; 371, 373–375, 379; 372; 381–382; 383–387; 21, 27, 31, 39. To deflate the series on research and development expenditures, a weighted average of the consumer price index (49%) and the wholesale price index (51%) was chosen. These weights were based on the percentage of total research and development costs allocated to wages and to materials, supplies and other costs, respectively, in 1971.

Notes

Chapter 1

1. Figure 1.1 is taken from Stern and Maskus (1981). The information from 1977 and 1978 is cited from Aho and Carney (1979). The following two paragraphs in the text draw mainly from the latter study. It should be noted that the broad trends in manufacturing trade which are highlighted here do not change in any appreciable qualitative fashion when the trade figures are deflated to control for the effects of inflation.

2. These figures are from Aho and Carney (Aho and Carney, pp. 4–8). The various definitions they employ for "technology intensity" are listed therein, but they do not exactly coincide with Hufbauer and Chilas' Product Cycle designation.

3. We also examine movements in the technology intensity of manufacturing trade by virtue of experiments performed on a restricted data set.

Chapter 2

1. See, for example, Deardorff (1979). Numerous attempts have been made to generalize the Heckscher-Ohlin proposition in terms of the numbers of goods, factors, and countries considered in the model. The primary articles are Melvin (1968) and Vanek (1968). The most recent, and least restrictive in terms of its assumptions, is Deardorff (1982) which examines the structure of the factor content of international trade in terms of the correlations between relative autarky factor prices and trade by factor.

2. We make no attempt here to summarize this vast literature. For useful reviews, see Stern (1975) or Hufbauer (1970).

3. Or it implies that capital inputs are not homogeneous, depending on the viewpoint taken. This does not necessarily invalidate the Heckscher-Ohlin notion of homogeneous factors across countries since we merely need to define a larger number of qualitatively identical factors which may be found in greater or lesser supplies across trading partners.

4. Indeed, this issue has become something of a controversy. See especially Baldwin (1971), Harkness and Kyle (1975), Branson and Monoyios (1977), and Stern and Maskus (1981).

5. This brief description by no means does justice to the full richness of the dynamic Product Cycle models (see especially Vernon, 1966, and Hirsch, 1967). The neo-technology account may also be depicted in terms of the "technology gap" models in which the lags between innovation and imitation of a new product give rise to trade. The notions are clearly similar.

6. Although, as Hufbauer (1970) pointed out, small, rich countries with ready access to large markets may export scale economy products as well. This seems to be the case for Denmark,

The Netherlands, and Sweden, all of which tend to be industrial style-setters, attaining scale economies through exports.

7. By "rankings" we mean that the goods may be ordered such that all goods below (above) a certain "rank" will be exported (imported). See also Travis (1972).

8. The list of market imperfections that may potentially influence the pattern of trade is virtually endless. The idea here is to specify those factors which are most likely to have induced shifts in the factor content of trade over the last two decades and about which we may have some information.

9. Baldwin (1971) argues that studies of the factor content of trade should focus on total (direct plus indirect) inputs by industry. However, for reasons specified in Batra and Casas (1973) and Krueger (1977) an emphasis on direct inputs into manufacturing industries may be more appropriate for regression analyses.

10. Although we will have occasion to consider separately the characteristics of a group of "natural-resource" manufacturing industries for reasons specified in chapter 3.

11. However, in an appendix we will attempt to explore the consequences of these exclusions for the efficacy of the estimates of the coefficients of the retained variables.

12. Certain empirical details, such as construction of variables and methods of deflation, are discussed in later chapters.

13. Bowen (1980b) does, however, provide some data on the accumulation of certain productive factors by 34 countries between 1963 and 1975. This information will be helpful in the interpretation of the results of the current study.

14. More will be said about this later.

15. The technology variables in the two forms of equation (2.3) will also be scaled by real shipments. The resulting variables will represent "technology intensity" by industry.

16. See, for example, Baldwin (1971) and Harkness and Kyle (1975).

17. It should be stressed that, as a measure of comparative advantage, exports divided by domestic output leaves much to be desired. An industry may export a smaller than average proportion of its output and still have a distinct comparative advantage in producing the product. Indeed, such is the description of an industry which finds itself at the beginning of the product life cycle; it may have been concentrating on introducing the good to the domestic market and only recently began exporting the good.

18. This is simply another way of explaining why exports minus imports forms a reasonable measure of comparative advantage, especially in the neo-factor proportions sense, while exports and imports separately may not. It also provides an intuitive explanation for the fact that "market structure" variables such as scale economies and resistance factors often show up as important in studies which focus on the export or import pattern alone, while they generally do not perform well in net exports equations. See Hufbauer (1970), Leamer (1974), Baldwin (1971, 1972), and Weiser and Jay (1972).

19. For various reasons there may be instances in which not all six models will be examined in detail.

20. Notice that scaling considerably aids us in the interpretation of the pooled coefficients. Consider, for example, a regression over time of the levels of real imports on the levels of factor inputs. In this case, secularly declining industries would tend to experience rising imports simultaneously with falling employment. On this score alone the pooled labor

coefficient might be expected to be negative even if the labor coefficients were positive in the annual cross-sections. This effect can be unrelated to factor intensities and endowments and consequently our conclusions with regard to the evolution of comparative advantage and the like may be unwarranted. Scaling by industry size or consumption to incorporate factor intensities into the analysis mitigates the problem, however, as discussed in the sequel.

21. Stern (1975) provides an informative review of the articles which appeared in this vein prior to 1973. Many such studies have been published since that time; in addition to the references previously cited in this chapter, important works include Goodman and Ceyhun (1976), Baldwin (1979), Lowinger (1975a), and Balassa (1979).

22. They also compared on a bilateral basis the characteristics of U.S., Japanese, and German trade with common third markets. Here the human capital intensity of U.S. exports asserted itself, but the labor coefficient was unchanged in sign or significance.

23. Japan, on the other hand, exhibited an increase in the technology intensity of its exports performance, perhaps reflecting the continuing maturation of that economy. In general, the Japanese coefficients exhibited the most instability as Japan "caught up with" or conformed with the American industrial structure.

24. See Heller (1976) for an analysis of Japan's trade structure along these lines. Heller concluded that changes in Japan's resource endowments between 1956 and 1969 were instrumental in shaping the course of its comparative advantage.

25. The interpretation of these simple models is always rendered rather difficult by the problem of omitted variables. We will have occasion to examine this issue more carefully in an appendix.

Chapter 3

1. Scaling by industry output implies that we expect, say, net exports to vary proportionately with industry size. However, if the relationship between net exports and industry size were nonlinear, as might be the case if the process is characterized by scale economies, then dividing by shipments could either overcorrect or not correct enough for the problem of scale economies.

2. In no case were any further adjustments indicated for the exports equations. In a few instances both the net exports and imports equations gave evidence of having been overcorrected, that is, the original scaling imposed an inverse relationship between the variance of the regression residuals and industry size. Since it was desired to maintain consistency among years, and since the untransformed scaled models make intuitive sense, it was decided to ignore these corrections throughout.

3. Since scaling by industry shipments (or consumption) served to eliminate heteroskedasticity in the bulk of the annual data samples, no further corrections were made on this account in the pooled samples. The pooled data sets are, however, adjusted for first-order serial correlation by industry.

4. It should be pointed out that it is possible that this characteristic of gradual trends may simply reflect the difficulty of discerning abrupt changes in the regression schemes in such a large data set. That is, since the coefficients represent averages over the pooled sub-periods, any marginal changes in the coefficients which result from shifting the sample splitting point are likely to be outweighed by the effects of the preponderance of observations in the pooled sub-samples.

5. Although note that the data transformations adopted in the pooled cases make them not strictly comparable with the unpooled cases. The R^2 values reported in table 3.5 were computed as the ratio of the regression sum of squares to the total sum of squares.

6. It should be mentioned that, since our variables are scale-free, the E scheme is probably the more appropriate one to use. Hence, if there exist cases in which the two schemes give markedly different results, we employ the E findings as the more suggestive of the two.

7. The fact that the CUSUM of SQUARES tests found more evidence of change than the CUSUM tests should perhaps occasion no surprise. The former tests are more sensitive to haphazard, jagged forms of structural change while the latter tests are better suited to identify gradual shifts. Figure 3.1 indicated that the changes in the exports equation were somewhat more haphazard than those in the net exports and imports equations.

8. The United States International Trade Commission, in its "Industrial Characteristics and Trade Performance Data Bank," lists as a natural resource measure the percent of total industry inputs purchased from mining and agriculture in 1973. Our set of Ricardo goods includes the top 22 natural-resource industries by this measure.

9. Since TECH goods are supposed to embody an advanced technology, it is possible that the human capital input in this group acted as a proxy for technological inputs. Some efforts at resolving this issue will be made in the next section.

10. In the tests comparing the annual cross-section regressions, none of the Ricardo coefficients registered significant changes. There were weak indications of an increase (decrease) in the physical capital intensity of TECH net exports (imports).

11. Indeed, both of these coefficients went up significantly over the period. The Ricardo exports capital coefficient was much smaller than the imports coefficient in the early part of the period, but the gap narrowed by the end of the period, giving a crude indication that the capital intensity of natural-resource industries exports tended to "catch up" with that of imports. While this is by no means a test of such an hypothesis, these trends, if true, in conjunction with the fact noted in chapter 1 that Ricardo goods trade has declined markedly in importance relative to total U.S. manufacturing trade, would help to explain the observed reversal by 1972 of the Leontief paradox (Stern and Maskus, 1981).

12. Details are deferred to the appendices.

13. The change in the L coefficient between 1958 and 1976 was significant, while the change in the H coefficient was not.

14. Cross-section regressions were run on the technology models excluding human capital, which tended to restore the significance of raw labor to some extent. The RD and ES variables took on the role of the human capital variable to a great extent in these regressions and were accordingly positive and highly significant in the net exports regressions, for example. Again, these results point up the difficulty of distinguishing between the neo-factor proportions and the neo-technology accounts of comparative advantage in small samples. Finally, it should be pointed out that multicollinearity may be present in the sample even if the correlations between any two variables are rather small; our experiments indicated that the existence of multicollinearity was primarily due to the high correlations between H on the one hand, and RD and ES on the other.

15. Results of the exports and imports equations are available upon request.

16. These results apparently are not strictly due to pooling over time, for recall from table 3.14 that the L and H coefficients changed signs in the 1970s in the cross-section regressions. Nor

are they due simply to the inclusion of ES for the signs of the variables of the ES-exclusive regressions changed as well. They would appear to be an artifact of the aggregation involved.

17. A possible explanation might be that the previously noted coefficient changes represented the effects of technological progress in the production of net exports which had proceeded relatively rapidly in the U.S. The introduction of the ES variable may have caused it to absorb the effects of the technological progress, since presumably it would be highly correlated over time with any such trends.

Chapter 4

1. A possible exception is the disaggregated exports equation.

2. Clearly, a problem surfaces at this point. The discussion thus far substantially assumes that an increase in the relative abundance of one factor will be reflected primarily in the implicit exchange of that factor's services alone, as reflected by the corresponding regression coefficient. This assumption suffers since an increase in the abundance of one factor implies a relative decline in the other factors, and this should show up in the latter coefficients. A rise in human capital abundance relative to a fixed raw labor supply is itself likely to cause a downward trend in the raw labor coefficient in the net exports equations, for example, as the latter factor becomes disadvantaged in trade. We largely ignore these "secondary" effects but the caveat should be kept in mind.

3. The U.S. has also experienced an increase in the relative supply of arable land, a factor which we have largely ignored by virtue of our focus on trade in manufactured goods.

4. The measures are somewhat different, both in concept and in fact, so the results are not strictly comparable.

5. Bowen also claimed that the ratio of skilled to total labor services in U.S. manufactured imports rose over the period, a result which was not supported by our regressions.

6. Total LDC manufactured exports to the U.S. rose from $3.6 billion in 1970 to $17.3 billion in 1977, which represented an increase in the LDC share of U.S. manufactured imports (relative to the share of other DCs) from 13.7 percent to 25.8 percent. U.S. manufactured exports to LDC markets have also risen over the period, but at a slower rate with the result that the U.S. share of total LDC imports of manufactured goods has declined from 34.0 percent in 1962 to 26.1 percent in 1979. On the other hand, the LDC's share of total U.S. exports rose from 31 percent in 1972 to 37 percent in 1979.

7. Although it is possible that some production characteristic applies to TECH goods which does not hold for U.S. industry on average. A consistently high degree of complementarity between skilled labor and physical capital in the production of TECH goods could explain the positive and significant signs on K, H, DUMK, and DUMH in equations (3.31) and (3.32), for example. Indeed, it has generally been found in the literature that K and H are complements (Stern, 1976). The picture which emerges, then, is one in which technological innovativeness (as measured by high research and development effort) is accompanied by relatively high capital intensity in those industries which, to a large extent, represent the greatest area of U.S. comparative advantage. This interpretation conflicts with the findings of Gruber, Mehta, and Vernon (1967) who found research and development effort to be negatively correlated with capital intensity.

8. Although some doubts have been expressed about these findings since Travis employed only a two-factor model.

9. Even so, the list of goods which have been subject to restrictions or distortions either in the U.S. or abroad is quite long. Some of the major industries on this list are agriculture, fishing, shipping and shipbuilding, railroads, air transportation, coal, petroleum, steel, nonferrous metals, cotton textiles, paper and pulp, electronics, aircraft, and transportation equipment. In addition, high technology and human capital-intensive goods are often subject to discriminatory government procurement policies (Baldwin, 1970).

10. Of course, the most current set of negotiations, the Tokyo Round, has the most important implications for the future patterns of world trade, especially since these negotiations are more attuned to the need for dismantling the various NTBs. However, the effects of these agreements would probably have little effect on the regression results detailed here, since our sample period ends at 1976. We thus make no further mention of the Tokyo Round here, other than perhaps to point out the likely results of their implementation, given our research results.

11. See Jackson (1977), Kreinin (1967), and Baldwin (1970). These early sessions focused on the reduction of tariffs, but to a great extent they succeeded only in removing a great deal of "water," or excessively high rates, from the tariff structures of the advanced countries with only a small amount of trade being affected. Once this was accomplished, it was recognized not only that further tariff cuts would begin to influence trade somewhat, but that the major remaining barriers to trade were NTBs such as quantitative import restrictions. The principle of eliminating such restrictions was established, if not followed very closely, at the Kennedy Round.

12. Although trade liberalization was certainly a contributing factor, we should emphasize that endowment changes and the associated industrialization were necessary to bring about the increases in LDC production and trade.

13. See Melvin (1979) and Ruttenberg (1978).

14. Some reforms of these acts were adopted in 1975 and 1976, although apparently the reforms have had little effect thus far (Ruttenberg).

15. (Ruttenberg, p. 118). It should be pointed out that some of this direct foreign investment has been offset by the direct investments of foreign firms in the U.S., a phenomenon which also is growing.

16. In this regard, it is worth pointing out that while U.S. comparative advantage continues to lie predominantly in the human capital-intensive sectors, Bowen's (1980b) evidence suggested that the relative U.S. abundance of skilled or educated labor may have slipped somewhat in recent years. On this basis it would seem ill-advised for policymakers to dismantle American programs which foster the formation of human capital.

17. We do not, however, ignore the results of the three-factor models, for these were estimated from a far more disaggregated data set than were the technology-variable-inclusive models.

18. Ruttenberg (1978), p. 139.

Appendix A

1. The pooled model presents a generalization of the usual varying-parameter models. In these, a single set of observations is ordered by some appropriate external variable, usually time, and the parameters which result from regression analysis are subjected to a variety of significance tests for nonconstancy. The choice of tests depends on the assumptions made about the forms which the parameter variations may take. For useful reviews, see Maddala (1977) and Goldfeld and Quandt (1973).

2. It should be pointed out that Quandt advanced this suggestion for a simple time-series context rather than a pooled situation. There is no problem, however, since the MLEs of the regression parameters are still their OLS counterparts, conditional on t^*. Notice also that this procedure is easily extended to allow for 2, 3, ..., m discrete switches, so long as one knows m beforehand.

3. Quandt (1958, 1960) claims that, letting ln λ denote the ratio of these log-likelihoods, the quantity $-\ln \lambda$ may be used as an indication of overall structural change in the relationship. There are serious problems with this contention, however, and this test will not be adopted here.

4. Although if the sample is split at the point indicated by the Quandt technique, the resulting statistic will not be distributed exactly as F.

5. It should be pointed out that the CUSUM techniques were not explicitly developed for the analysis of unconcentrated or repeated structural change, although they have been used for this purpose in the past (Stern, Baum, and Greene, 1979). Some attempts have been made at developing tests for gradual movements in regression parameters. See Tsurumi and Tsurumi (1980), Goldfeld and Quandt (1973), and the references cited in Maddala (chapter 17).

Appendix B

1. If X_1 and X_2 are stochastic, a similar statement applies with regard to both small-sample and asymptotic bias. Hence, in neither case do the biases disappear as sample size is increased.

2. We emphasize that these results should be treated with caution. The industry coverage in these 1960 and 1970 cross-sections is much less than that of the analysis in the body of the book, at least with regard to the three-factor model. More importantly, the years 1960 and 1970 are really not that far removed from each other when considered in the context of the kinds of structural changes which are suspected to exist here. Many of the shifts noted in the annual cross-sections in chapter 3, for example, were significant only when 1958 was compared with 1976. Several of the coefficient changes in the current tariff-inclusive model were in fact "nearly significant," with a decline in the raw labor intensity of net exports (22% level of significance) and an increase in the physical capital intensity (16%). We suspect that these shifts would be registered more strongly if the two years of comparison had been more widely separated.

Bibliography

Aho, C.M. and Carney, R.D. "An Empirical Analysis of the Structure of U.S. Manufacturing Trade, 1965–1976." Economic Discussion Paper 3, U.S. Department of Labor, Bureau of International Labor Affairs (1979).

———, and Rosen, H.F. "Trends in Technology-Intensive Trade: With Special Reference to U.S. Competitiveness." Office of Foreign Economic Research, Bureau of International Labor Affairs, U.S. Department of Labor (1980).

Balassa, B. "The Changing Pattern of Comparative Advantage in Manufactured Goods." *Review of Economics and Statistics* Vol. 61 (1979): pp. 259–66.

Baldwin, R.E. *Nontariff Distortions of International Trade.* Washington, DC: The Brookings Institution (1970).

———. "Determinants of the Commodity Structure of U.S. Trade." *American Economic Review* Vol. 61 (1971): pp. 126–46.

———. "Determinants of the Commodity Structure of U.S. Trade: Reply." *American Economic Review* Vol. 62 (1972): p. 465.

———. "Determinants of Trade and Foreign Investment: Further Evidence." *Review of Economics and Statistics* Vol. 61 (1979): pp. 40–48.

Batra, R.N. and Casas, F.R. "Intermediate Products and the Pure Theory of International Trade: A Neo-Heckscher-Ohlin Framework." *American Economic Review* Vol. 63 (1973): pp. 297–311.

Bowen, H.P. "Resources, Technology, and Dynamic Comparative Advantage: A Cross-Country Analysis of the Product Cycle Theory of International Trade." Unpublished Ph.D. Dissertation, UCLA (1980a).

———. "Changes in the International Pattern of Factor Abundance and the Composition of Trade: A Multi-Country Analysis of Changing Comparative Advantage in Manufactured Goods with Special Reference to the United States." Office of Foreign Economic Research, Bureau of International Labor Affairs, U.S. Department of Labor (1980b).

Branson, W.H. "U.S. Comparative Advantage: Some Further Results." *Brookings Papers on Economic Activity* 3 (1971): pp. 754–59.

———, and Junz, H.B. "Trends in U.S. Trade and Comparative Advantage." *Brookings Papers on Economic Activity* 2 (1971): pp. 285–338.

———, and Monoyios, N. "Factor Inputs in U.S. Trade." *Journal of International Economics* Vol. 7 (1977): pp. 111–31.

Brown, R.L. and Durbin, J. "Methods of Investigating whether a Regression Relationship is Constant Over Time." *Selected Statistical Papers 1: European Meeting 1968, Amsterdam Mathematical Centre Tracts* Vol. 26 (1968): pp. 37–45.

———, Durbin, J. and Evans, J.M. "Techniques for Testing the Constancy of Regression Relationships Over Time," *Journal of Royal Statistical Society,* Series B Vol. 37 (1975): pp. 149-92.

Deardorff, A.V. "Weak Links in the Chain of Comparative Advantage." *Journal of International Economics* Vol. 9 (1979): pp. 197–210.

_____. "The General Validity of the Heckscher-Ohlin Theorem." *American Economic Review* Vol. 72 (1982): pp. 638–94.

Goldfeld, S.M. and Quandt, R.E. *Nonlinear Methods in Econometrics.* Amsterdam, The Netherlands: North-Holland (1975).

Goodman, B. and Ceyhun, F. "U.S. Export Performance in Manufacturing Industries: An Empirical Investigation." *Weltwirtschaftliches Archiv* Vol. 112 (1976): pp. 525–55.

Gruber, W., Mehta, D., and Vernon, R. "The R&D Factor in International Trade and International Investment of United States Industries." *Journal of Political Economy* Vol. 75 (1967): pp. 20–37.

Harkness, J. "Factor Abundance and Comparative Advantage." *American Economic Review* Vol. 68 (1978): pp. 784–800.

_____, and Kyle, J.F. "Factors Influencing United States Comparative Advantage." *Journal of International Economics* Vol. 5 (1975): pp. 153–66.

Heller, R.S. "Factor Endowment Change and Comparative Advantage: The Case of Japan, 1959–1969." *Review of Economics and Statistics* Vol. 58 (1976): pp. 283–92.

Hirsch, S. *Location of Industry and International Competitiveness.* Oxford, Great Britain: The Clarendon University Press (1967).

Hufbauer, G.C. "The Impact of National Characteristics and Technology on the Commodity Composition of Trade in Manufactured Goods." *The Technology Factor in World Trade,* edited by R. Vernon. New York: Columbia University Press (1970).

_____, and Chilas, J.G. "Specialization by Industrial Countries: Extent and Consequences." *The International Division of Labor: Problems and Prospects,* edited by H. Giersch. Tubingen, Federal Republic of Germany: J.C.B. Mohr (1974).

Jackson, J.H. *Legal Problems of International Economic Relations: Cases, Materials and Text.* St. Paul, MN: American Casebook Series, West Publishing Co. (1977).

Johnston, J. *Econometric Methods.* New York: McGraw-Hill (1972).

Klein, R.W. "A Dynamic Theory of Comparative Advantage." *American Economic Review* Vol. 63 (1973): pp. 173–84.

Kmenta, J. *Elements of Econometrics.* New York: Macmillan (1971).

Kreinin, M.E. *Alternative Commercial Policies: Their Effect on the American Economy.* East Lansing, MI: MSU International Business and Economic Studies (1967).

Krueger, A.O. "Growth, Distortions, and Patterns of Trade among Many Countries." *Princeton Studies in International Finance* No. 40 (1977).

Leamer, E.E. "The Commodity Composition of International Trade in Manufactures: An Empirical Analysis." *Oxford Economic Papers* Vol. 26 (1974): pp. 350–74.

_____. "A Study of Comparative Advantage with Emphasis on Labor's Interest." Unpublished manuscript (1980).

_____, and Bowen, H.P. "Cross-Section Tests of the Heckscher-Ohlin Theorem: A Methodological Comment." *American Economic Review* Vol. 71 (1981): pp. 1040–43.

Leontief, W. "Domestic Production and Foreign Trade: The American Capital Position Re-examined." *Proceedings of the American Philosophical Society* Vol. 97 (1953): pp. 332–49.

_____. "Factor Proportions and the Structure of American Trade: Further Theoretical and Empirical Analysis." *Review of Economics and Statistics* Vol. 38 (1956): pp. 386–407.

Lowinger, T.C. "The Technology Factor and the Export Performance of U.S. Manufacturing Industries." *Economic Inquiry* Vol. 13 (1975a): pp. 221–36.

_____. "Human Capital and Technological Determinants of U.S. Industries' Revealed Comparative Advantage." Unpublished manuscript (1975b).

Madalla, G.S. *Econometrics.* New York: McGraw-Hill (1977).

Melvin, J.R. "Production and Trade with Two Factors and Three Goods." *American Economic Review* Vol. 58 (1968): pp. 1249–68.

————. "Commodity Taxation as a Determinant of Trade." *Canadian Journal of Economics* Vol. 3 (1970): pp. 62–78.

————. "Short-Run Price Effects of the Corporate Income Tax and Implications for International Trade." *American Economic Review* Vol. 69 (1979): pp. 765–74.

Mitchell, D.J.B. "Recent Changes in the Labor Content of U.S. International Trade." *Industrial and Labor Relations Review* Vol. 28 (1975): pp. 355–75.

Quandt, R.E. "The Estimation of the Parameters of a Linear Regression System Obeying Two Separate Regimes." *Journal of the American Statistical Association* Vol. 53 (1958): pp. 873–80.

————. "Tests of the Hypothesis that a Linear Regression System Obeys Two Separate Regimes." *Journal of the American Statistical Association* Vol. 55 (1960): pp. 324–30.

Ruttenberg, S.H. "The Impact of "Manufacturing Trade on Employment." *Trade and Employment*, Special Report of the National Commission for Manpower Policy No. 30, Washington, DC (1978).

Stern, R.M. "Testing Trade Theories." *International Trade and Finance: Frontiers for Research*, edited by P.B. Kenen. Cambridge, MA: Cambridge University Press (1975).

————. "Capital-Skill Complementarity and U.S. Trade in Manufactures." *Quantitative Studies of International Economic Relations*, edited by H. Glejser. Amsterdam, The Netherlands: North-Holland Publishing Co. (1976a).

————. Some Evidence on the Factor Content of West Germany's Foreign Trade." *Journal of Political Economy* Vol. 84 (1976b), pp. 131–41.

————. "Changes in U.S. Comparative Advantage: Issues for Research and Policy." Paper presented at the National Science Foundation Colloquium on International Economic Policy, Washington, DC (1980).

————, Baum, C.F., and Greene, M.N. "Evidence on Structural Change in the Demand for Aggregate U.S. Imports and Exports." *Journal of Political Economy* Vol. 87 (1979): pp. 179–92.

————, and Maskus, K.E. "Determinants of the Structure of U.S. Foreign Trade, 1958–76." *Journal of International Economics* Vol. 11 (1981): pp. 207–24.

Travis, W.P. "Production, Trade, and Protection when There Are Many Commodities and Two Factors." *American Economic Review* Vol. 62 (1972): pp. 87–106.

Tsurumi, H. and Tsurumi, Y. "A Bayesian Test of the Product Life Cycle as Applied to the U.S. Demand for Color-TV Sets." *International Economic Review* Vol. 21 (1980): pp. 583–97.

United States Senate Committee on Banking, Housing, and Urban Affairs. *Export Promotion, Export Disincentives, and U.S. Competitiveness*, Washington, DC: U.S. Government Printing Office (1980).

Vanek, J. "The Factor-Proportions Theory: The N-Factor Case." *Kyklos* Vol. 21 (1968): pp. 749–56.

Vernon, R. "International Investment and International Trade in the Product Life Cycle." *Quarterly Journal of Economics* Vol. 80 (1966): pp. 190–207.

Weiser, L.A. "Changing Factor Requirements of United States Foreign Trade." *Review of Economics and Statistics* Vol. 50 (1968): pp. 356–60.

————, and Jay, K. "Determinants of the Commodity Structure of U.S. Trade: Comment." *American Economic Review* Vol. 62 (1972): pp. 459–64.

Index